Child and Adolescent Psychotherapy

Child and Adolescent Psychotherapy

Wounded Spirits and Healing Paths

David A. Crenshaw

JASON ARONSON

Lanham • Boulder • New York • Toronto • Plymouth, UK

LEXINGTON BOOKS

A division of Rowman & Littlefield Publishers, Inc.
A wholly owned subsidiary of The Rowman & Littlefield Publishing Group, Inc.
4501 Forbes Boulevard, Suite 200
Lanham, MD 20706

Estover Road
Plymouth PL6 7PY
United Kingdom

British Library Cataloguing in Publication Information Available

Library of Congress Cataloging-in-Publication Data

Crenshaw, David A.
  Child and adolescent psychotherapy : wounded spirits and healing paths /
David A. Crenshaw.
      p. ; cm.
  Includes bibliographical references and index.
  1. Child psychotherapy. 2. Adolescent psychotherapy. I. Title.
  [DNLM: 1. Child. 2. Psychotherapy—methods. 3. Adolescent. 4.
  Psychotherapeutic Processes. 5. Stress Disorders, Traumatic—therapy.
  WS 350.2 C915c 2008]

  RJ504.C738 2008
  618.92'8914—dc22   08032563

ISBN: 978-0-7657-0598-3 (cloth : alk. paper)
ISBN: 978-0-7657-0599-0 (pbk. : alk. paper)
ISBN: 978-0-7657-0609-6 (electronic)

Printed in the United States of America

DEDICATION

In my clinical work and writing, I stand on the shoulders of giants in the field who have taught me and inspired me more than they can ever know. No one among those giants stands taller than James Garbarino. Currently, Professor and Maude C. Clarke Chair in Humanistic Psychology at Loyola University, and Director of the Center for the Human Rights of Children at Loyola, Garbarino is the author of more than twenty books.

Referred to by Edward Zigler as one of the nation's major social critics, his groundbreaking research and writing on children in refugee camps around the world, his study of children growing up in war zones from Cambodia, Mozambique, Kuwait, Nicaragua, and Palestine, not to mention his work with children growing up in this country in inner city war zones has influenced a whole generation of child development specialists, mental health professionals, politicians, and policy makers.

Garbarino's book, *Lost Boys: Why Our Sons Turn Violent and How We Can Save Them* is destined to be a classic in the field and makes a compelling case for viewing in a humanistic way those youth who suffer traumatic, often unrecognized and untreated slashes to the soul that ultimately lead to a huge cost to society not just economically but more poignantly in pain and suffering. The imperiled youth of today's world facing both environmental and social toxicity on a scale never seen prior are fortunate to have in their corner, a man so eloquent in prose, so compassionate of heart, so astute and insightful, and unwaveringly passionate in his advocacy for them, as James Garbarino. It is little wonder that immediately after the cease-fire in the Persian Gulf War; Garbarino was called upon to go to Kuwait by UNICEF to help the children cope with the trauma of war.

James Garbarino was, prior to taking his current position, President of the Erikson Institute for Advanced Study in Child Development in Chicago and Co-Director of the Family Life Development Center and Professor of Human Development at Cornell University. Every now and then among the giants of the field emerges someone of incomparable commitment, so gifted, with a heart so big, that the field is changed forever. James Garbarino is surely one of those persons.

Contents

Acknowledgements

It is quite special when I can collaborate in a writing project with contributing authors for whom I hold great affection and respect. I especially wish to acknowledge the enormous influence on my career of the writings and teachings of James Garbarino and Kenneth V. Hardy. Their work has both informed and inspired my clinical work and writing. Andrew Fussner has been a good friend for eighteen years. He is an extraordinary teacher in the family therapy field and I have learned most of what I know about family therapy from him. All of the contributing authors share a passion for the work that we do and a common bond in our shared conviction that both children and families deserve nothing less than our best efforts and skills to help, in the context of a profound respect for their dignity as human beings. The contributing authors in this book also share the view that children and teens as well as their families bring important strengths into the therapy room and that appreciation of those talents, positive personal qualities, as well as their courage and determination provide the best leverage for facilitating change. It is not the strengths and talents of the therapist but of the child and family that we seek to honor.

1

Multiple Sources of Child Wounding and Paths to Healing

David A. Crenshaw

OVERVIEW

This introductory chapter discusses the myriad ways of child wounding in today's world and multiple paths of healing the injuries to the soul. The chapters to follow discuss some of the clinical implications and applications of relational approaches to healing the crushed spirit of a child including wounds to our children related to multiple losses and trauma, often disguised by rage. Healing within a family context, the importance of a strengths-based approach and pursuing the powerful theme of seeking a "shelter for the soul" are also explored in later chapters. The necessity of the therapist's own healing process before undertaking the healing of others is the focus of a subsequent chapter. The introductory chapter lays the theoretical foundation for the clinical applications that follow.

How many times can a child's heart be shattered and the pieces still put back together? How often can the wondrous spirit of children be crushed and still bounce back? What does it take to extinguish the "divine spark" (Garbarino, 1999) in youth so that the flame of hope, of passion, of dreams goes out? Wounds to the spirit cut deep to the core of what makes the child essentially and uniquely human and the pain is devastating. Hegel's (1979) memorable sentence in the *Phenomenology of Spirit* stated, "The wounds of the spirit heal and leave no scars behind" (p. 407). While this is a hopeful message and true in one sense, it may be misleading because wounds to the spirit of the child are harder to heal than physical injuries because the soul of the child is often crushed along the way. Physical wounds are often more respected and honored than wounds to the soul that, at best, are often unrecognized and, at worst, devalued. Healing occurs in relation to an

1

empathic healer committed to accompany the child through the thicket of invisible wounds, losses beyond words, searing pain, profound sorrow, and intense rage. It requires perseverance, courage, and determination on the part of both the child and therapist.

In this book the terms soul and spirit will be used interchangeably. What I mean by the soul or the spirit is the unique and special essence that makes a person more than the sum total of its biological composition consisting of DNA, RNA proteins, lipids and sugars, water and carbon dioxide, oxygen, carbon, hydrogen, nitrogen, salts, calcium, iron, and sulfur and other elements. In addition, I view human beings as capable of being inspired to a higher purpose and in contrast to animal life they are able to seek meaning in their life pursuits that go beyond satisfying biological needs or material desires. The unique essence of the human person that distinguishes us from all other creatures is this quest for deeper meaning and purpose, our ability to be inspired and moved by music, poetry, art, altruistic causes, the joy of giving that trumps the pleasure of receiving, and the appreciation of beauty. Readers may view these awe-inspiring qualities in different ways and name them differently, some will use a religious or faith-based framework for understanding, what I am calling the soul or the spirit of a child. It definitely falls into the realm of the spiritual because it can never be adequately explained in material terms.

In the Spring of 2007 in Corning, NY, I was honored to be on the same program titled "Restoring Hope, Light, and Dignity in the Lives of Abused and Traumatized Children" with Raffi Cavoukian, the children's troubadour, known by millions of families throughout the world for his unique ability to capture the heart of childhood. Raffi credits Nelson Mandela and the Dalai Lama for the inspiration to develop a bold initiative, which he calls *Child Honoring*. Child Honoring is informed by the pioneering work of child psychiatrist, Stanley Greenspan (Greenspan & Shanker, 2006) and many others who have identified the crucial importance of the experiences of early childhood on human development. Raffia's stated, "Across all cultures, we find an essential humanity that is most visible in early childhood—a playful, intelligent, and creative way of being. Early experience lasts a lifetime. It shapes our sense of self and how we see others; it also shapes our sense of what's possible, our emerging view of the world" (Cavoukian and Olfman, 2006, p. xviii). Raffia's message is one of deep concern that children who represent the best hope for the future of humanity are being born into a world that is increasingly socially and environmentally toxic.

Raffi described Child Honoring as a "Compassionate Revolution." A key premise of Child Honoring is explained by Raffi, "Children who feel seen, loved, and honored are far more able to become loving parents and productive citizens. Children who do not feel valued are disproportionately represented on welfare rolls and police records. Much of the criminal justice system deals with the results of childhood wounding (the vast majority of sexual offenders, for example, were themselves violated as children), and much of the social service sector represents an attempt to rectify or moderate this damage, which comes at an enormous cost to society. Most of the correctional work is too little, too late" (Cavoukian and Olfman, 2006, pp. xix–xx).

Insults to the spirit of our youth take many forms and so do the paths to healing. The wide spectrum of biological, psychological, social, environmental, and cultural stressors that impinge on our young people as they traverse the path from infancy to adulthood demands flexible, comprehensive, and carefully reasoned healing approaches. Above all, in an increasing depersonalized world, healing of our youth calls for a relational approach based on empathy, compassion, authentic interest and commitment, if we are to reach our most troubled and troubling youth.

Some of the contemporary sources of injuries to the soul, and alienation among our youth are identified in the first part of this chapter followed by various relational theoretical approaches that inform the clinical work and stories of healing to be told in subsequent chapters. (For ease of communication, throughout this book, children and youth will be used to refer to both school-age children and teens unless otherwise specified.)

ANGUISH IN THE HEARTS OF CHILDREN IN TODAY'S WORLD

A Multitude of Ways of Camouflaging Inner Torment

Children find countless ways to mask wounds to their spirit. Michael, age 15, is enraged at the world. He is no longer permitted to attend school because of his violent episodes and sees little prospects for his future. His only friends are in trouble as often as he. Sarah doesn't talk to anyone anymore except her boyfriend and two girl friends. At 14, she has given up on the adults in her life. Her primary objectives are to get high as often as possible and make sure adults do not run her life. Roberto is 7, and is already identified as a problem child in school. He shows no interest in schoolwork, nor does he experience any success with academic tasks. He is, however, a first-class bully and most of the kids in his grade fear him. Roberto tyrannizes them on the playground. Ross, at 16, is building up his credentials to qualify as an ultimate menace to society. He hates authority, has little or no respect for any adult; subscribes to the credo "hurt others before they hurt you," and he has lost his capacity to feel pain, either his own or the hurt of others.

Complications of the Camouflages

Most of the myriad ways that youth create to camouflage their inner torment merely complicate and deepen their emotional hurt. In addition to the time honored adolescent excesses related to alcohol and marijuana use, reckless driving, unsafe sexual practices, some use cocaine (powder, crack, or free-base), ecstasy, or methamphetamines. Smaller numbers of youth use heroin; or they may abuse prescription pain medications like Oxycontin (the choice of which clearly reveals their inner hurt); and still others sniff glue, or breathe the content of various aerosol spray cans or paint cans (O'Sullivan, 2005).

Gender Differences not in Suffering but in Camouflaging the Hurt

Some youth are considered internalizers who develop symptoms such as depression, anxiety, or eating disorders. Still others cut or burn themselves or make suicidal gestures or attempts. Fortunately, the overall rate of suicide among youth has declined slowly since 1992, but still remains unacceptably high with suicide the third leading cause of death in the age range 15 to 24 (Anderson & Smith, 2003). Girls are more likely to respond to the scarring of their spirit by internalizing symptoms (McGee & Baker, 2002; Ruchkin, Sukhodolsky, Vermeiren, Koposov, & Schwab-Stone, 2006).

Boys tend to externalize. Of course, there are always exceptions to these patterns but in response to degradation, humiliation, devaluation, disconnection, shame and repeated losses, boys are more likely than girls to act-out often by increased aggression and violence, or other forms of high risk behavior (McGee and Baker, 2002; Ruchkin, Sukhodolsky, Vermeiren, Koposov, & Schwab-Stone, 2006). Their aggressive behavior masks the emotional distress they suffer in shame and secrecy.

Garbarino (2006a) observed that this gender difference in recent years is declining with more girls acting-out in aggressive ways that in the past were more typical of boys. Hardy noted in a personal communication (August, 2005), that often we can't see past the ugliness of the violence, which neither he nor I condone, to see the devastating injuries to the spirit of our youth.

DISCONNECTION AND SPIRITUAL EMPTINESS

Looking to the Dark Side to Fill the Void

In the flat world described by Thomas Friedman (2006) of global electronic connectivity there is plenty of human disconnection among our youth. James Garbarino (1999) in his groundbreaking book, *Lost Boys*, discussed the spiritual emptiness of youth that leads some of our most troubled boys and girls to turn to the dark side of life to fill that void. They turn to illicit drugs, abuse alcohol, misuse prescription or over-the-counter drugs; engage in hypersexual activity in a misguided attempt to fill the unmet longings for satisfying human connection and to find some sense of peace in the bewilderment of their world, or to cope with the alienation, loneliness, and lack of meaning to their lives.

Peter Whybrow (2005) in *American Mania: When More Is not Enough* explained that the driven, frenzied pace of American contemporary life is making us sick as the obsessive pursuit of more and still more in the material realm interferes with satisfying human connections. Our preoccupation with consumption leaves little time or energy to nurture our vital relationships with family including our children, our loved ones and friends. Susan Linn (2006) reported on how commercialized media has overrun childhood. She noted that in 1983, corporations spent $100 million annually in direct advertising to children, but that has increased to 15 billion today.

HUNGER FOR A DEEPER PURPOSE AND MEANING

The longing for a deeper purpose and sense of meaningful belonging in the world has led to pursuit of ultimately unsatisfying substitutes in the form of materialism, status, and occupational prominence. Tim Kasser (2002) in a ground-breaking book, *The High Price of Materialism*, based on ten years of empirical research, revealed that people whose values center on the accumulation of wealth or material possessions face a greater risk of unhappiness, including anxiety, depression, low self-esteem, and problems with intimacy irrespective of age, income, or culture.

Kasser showed that materialistic values actually undermine our well-being, as they perpetuate feelings of insecurity, weaken the ties with those who are important to us, and make us feel less free. Thus, even children growing up in affluent families are sometimes enraged because they feel emotionally deprived and lonely; cut-off from connections with parents who are either physically or emotionally unavailable or both.

John O'Donohue (2000), the Irish poet and philosopher, in *Eternal Echoes*, stated, "Consumerist culture is not simply an outer frame that surrounds our lives. It is deeper and more penetrating than that. In fact it is a way of thinking that seeps into our minds and becomes a powerful inner compass. Consumerism and its greed are an awful perversion of our longing; they damage our ability to experience things. They clutter our lives with things we do not need and subvert our sense of priority" (p. 79). Likewise, Garbarino (2006b) in a lecture at Marist College told of interviewing an eighteen-year-old man who had been sentenced to life in prison. The young man told Garbarino, "My life is over." When Garbarino inquired further about his feelings, the young man explained, "I will never be able to go the mall again." How sad that far too many youth are being schooled in the values of rampant consumption and materialism to the point, in extreme cases, that there life becomes centered on a shopping mall.

THE SEXUALIZATION OF YOUNG GIRLS: AN ADDITIONAL FORM OF CULTURAL WOUNDING

Another feature of American culture that is damaging to the spirit of our youth is the sexualization of young girls. A task force of the American Psychological Association (APA; 2007) headed by Ellen L. Zurbriggen completed a two-year review of research related to this issue. The report indicates that "sexualization occurs when people value a woman or a girl primarily for her sexual appeal or behavior; hold her to a narrow standard of beauty; equate her physical beauty with sexiness; view her as an object for sexual use; or inappropriately impose sexuality on her" (American Psychological Association, Task Force on the Sexualization of Girls, 2007, p. 27).

The task force report shows that sexualization of women and girls in this country has intensified over time and that sexualization has a range of negative effects for young women, including the devaluing of their cognitive abilities, increased body shame, depression, eating disorders, and low self-esteem. The power of media, the advertising industry, teen magazines, music videos, music lyrics, movies, video games, and the internet to promote the image of girls looking "hot" and "sexy" for boys is documented by studies summarized in the APA Report.

Lukas (2004) and Lamb (2006) documented that girls are instructed by society to be compliant sexual objects. Children growing up today, whether girls or boys, are over- exposed by the media to sex. There is a huge commercial force behind this overexposure which includes "selling thongs sized for 7-to-10-year-old girls" (American Psychological Association, Task Force on the Sexualization of Girls, 2007, p. 1). Some of the effects of the sexualization of girls are insidious. The APA Task Force Report stated, "The sexualization and objectification of women in the media appear to teach girls that as women, all they have to offer is their body and face and that they should expend all their effort on physical appearance" (2007, p. 27). This is a narrow and devaluing way of regarding young women that sadly ignores completely their unique abilities, interests, personal qualities, and human potentials.

Among the recommendations of the APA Task Force for counteracting the cultural and media influence on sexualization are comprehensive educational programs and enlistment of the family to help girls filter and interpret sexualizing messages from the media in ways that reduce harm. In addition, direct work with girls and girls' groups founded on empowerment and appreciation of their value as persons in the world quite aside from their sexual appeal is recommended (American Psychological Association, Task Force on the Sexualization of Girls, 2007). In this regard, a beautiful and sensitive book written for young girls by Suzanne Haas-Cunningham (in press) at Syracuse University, called *The Princess Whose Heart Felt Empty*, addressed this very issue.

PUNITIVE APPROACHES:
A SUBTLE FORM OF CULTURAL TOXICITY

The toxic cultural factors that include extreme poverty, high crime neighborhoods, inadequate educational and employment opportunities, so well documented in writings by Garbarino (1995, 1999) and Hardy and Laszloffy (2005) while particularly devastating to young people living at the margins of a society have a long reach and impacted all socioeconomic groups as illustrated above in the sexualization of young girls. Currie (2004) in his book, *The Road to Whatever*, detailed the crisis of middle-class youth in today's culture. He notes the concerns about suburban school violence, rising drug and alcohol abuse, and reckless sex among middle-class youth. Currie observes that the "hidden deviance" among the more affluent adolescents of the suburbs was often lightly chalked up to misguided and indulgent liberal values. He notes, however this view, which enjoyed great popularity in the 1990s, ignored the reality of how youth were actually being treated in the United States.

Zero-tolerance policies toward juvenile misbehavior in schools led to suspension and/or expulsion of students for even relatively minor infractions. Severe penalties from new drug laws have put large numbers of youth in correctional institutions, often for protracted sentences. In addition, part of the crack down on youth crime entailed sending juvenile offenders to adult courts. Currie stated, "More generally, the United States had long been a country distinctive in the advanced industrial world for the harshness of its policies toward children and youth, and especially toward adolescent deviance. Where many other nations had formally abolished the use of corporal punishment of children in homes and schools, we had formally upheld it in the courts—and practiced it widely" (2004, p. 7). Those who advocate for more punitive approaches toward our young people tend to view it as a novel approach, when, in fact, as Anna Freud pointed out more than 60 years ago, it has been utilized repeatedly, and often severely.

RELATIONAL PATHS OF HEALING

The healing paths to be considered under the broad brush of Relational Therapy share in common the theme of focusing therapy on the important relationships in the child's life as well as on the therapeutic relationship. These therapy approaches are compatible with theoretical orientations that give emphasis to interpersonal, social, and cultural determinants of personality. Among the theories that emphasize relational factors are Relational Theory (DeYoung, 2003); Relational-Cultural Theory (Miller, 1978, 1986; Miller & Stiver, 1997); Relational Psychoanalysis (Mitchell and Aron, 2003, 1999); Culturalist Psychoanalysis (Bonime, 1989); Family Systems Theory (Minuchin & Fishman, 1981; Minuchin & Nichols, 1993); Attachment Theory (Benedict, 2006; Benedict & Hastings, 2002; Bowlby, 1988; Hughes, 1997, 2006, 2007) and Interpersonal Neurobiology Theory (Schore 1994, 2003a, 2003b; Siegel 1999, 2007).

A variety of therapeutic approaches that stress the critical importance of the client-therapist relationship can be grouped under the relational heading: Sullivan's interpersonal therapy; Fairbairn, Winnicott, and Klein's object relations work; Kohut's self-psychology; and, more recently, postmodern feminist approaches (Curtis & Hirsch, 2003; Raskin, 2007). Magnavita (2006) observed, "The relational matrix is the ultimate unifying principle of human development and of psychotherapy. It plays a central role in shaping and influencing human function and dysfunction" (p. 887).

In relational approaches to therapy the therapeutic relationship itself is examined closely for feelings and reactions evoked both in the child and the therapist. Bonime (1989) observed, "We strive to understand the nature of each patient as a person and to be as clear as possible about our subjective reaction to the uniqueness and immediacy of each patient during the course of therapy" (p. 376). Trauma, for example, is worked with clinically as it emerges in the relational field between child and therapist. In addition, in relational therapies, the importance of attending to ruptures and misunderstandings in the therapeutic relationship is central to the healing process (DeYoung, 2003). Chapter 9 focuses on the issue of the therapist healing oneself and working with the reactions stirred in clinical work on an ongoing basis.

Since this book is intended for clinicians, my aim is be as jargon free as possible, a skill that Bonime (1989) was well known for and also strongly advocated among his psychoanalytic colleagues. In fact, Bonime (1989) with his wife Florence, who was a writer, penned an essay on "Psychoanalytic Writing: An Essay on Communication" in which he advocated for writing that translates easily into "common speech." Unfortunately a significant degree of contemporary psychoanalytic relational theory is shrouded in mystifying jargon.

There is no "one size fits all" path to healing. The paths of healing, the theoretical orientations and therapy approaches outlined in the above paragraphs do not represent a comprehensive or exhaustive list of all the possible healing approaches but they encompass frameworks broad enough in scope to take into account both the internal life of the child along with the social, familial, and cultural context in which the child's development takes place and they emphasize respect for the strengths of the child and family as an essential healing factor. I will elaborate below on two of the potential healing paths that particularly shaped the rationale behind the selection and design for the chapters to follow in this book.

The Family System's Healing Path

Families are the primary human relational incubator that prepares us for interaction with the larger world. They are also one of the most potent of all human relational contexts for healing. Of course, if the family context is destructive, the wounds inflicted may lacerate the soul. But if the emotional slashes to the child's spirit are to be healed it often can be facilitated by enlisting the resources of the family.

Family systems therapy consists of contextualizing the presenting problem. Olga Silverstein (1987), now retired from the faculty of the Ackerman Institute for the Family, explained that she always set the context for the family work from the outset. She reframed the presenting problem so that it was *relational*; it was *purposeful*; it was something that they could have some *control over*. She used metaphors and stories; Silverstein skillfully weaved the problem story into a contextual story. The story would fit the family's own particular logic and often she would give the story a title. She saw language as a powerful tool in therapy and particularly stressed the power of positive connotation of symptoms and reframing. Olga Silverstein saw the art of systems family therapy as taking the disconnected stories and weaving them in such a way to reconstruct a new reality for the family.

Hardy in a presentation at the Ackerman Institute for the Family in December, 2005 stated, "There is a difference between treating and healing. Healing takes a lot longer" (Hardy, 2005). Waters and Lawrence (1993) in their competence-based approach to family therapy articulated the difference between quick fixes versus healing approaches in family therapy. They state, "Where a fixing approach tries to get a family out of therapy and back on the road as quickly as possible, a healing orientation is more interested in reaching people at a deeper level; healers worry less about the length of treatment and more about its depth. They go beyond the symptoms, for the information and intensity they contain, rather than just trying to dispel them. Healing involves going toward what hurts and accepting it with courage, *so that it may be let go*" (Waters and Lawrence, 1993, p. 13). The demand that the therapy we provide our youth be fast-paced and symptom-focused is a reflection of the mania in our culture that is antithetical to the health and healing of adults and young people alike (Marmot, 2006; McPherson, Brashears, & Smith-Lovin, 2006; and Rokach, 2004). Leslie Greenberg (2004) stated it succinctly, "You can't leave a place until you have arrived at it." Chapter 3 of this book discusses in detail the family system's path to healing.

THE CULTURALIST PSYCHOANALYTIC HEALING PATH

I learned the value of integrating the influences of psychodynamic, interpersonal and cultural factors as determinants of personality from Walter Bonime. Bonime (1962, 1989) was known as a Culturalist Psychoanalyst who integrated the methods of psychoanalytic therapy without the emphasis on psychosexual development of classical Freudians but rather explored a broader range of influences with special emphasis on interpersonal and cultural determinants. While using the Freudian tools of free association, dream analysis, and exploration of the therapeutic relationship, Bonime and others in the Culturalist group such as Karen Horney, Erich Fromm, and Frieda Fromm-Reichmann put the punctuation on sociocultural determinants of personality.

Alfred Adler is recognized as the first major dissenter from such a pronounced focus on libido theory and the first "Culturalist," who emphasized the critical importance of social connectedness for mental health (Bonime, 1989). Bonime became a candidate-in-training at the newly founded American Institute of Psychoanalysis in 1939 formed by Karen Horney, who was the first dean. Karen Horney and Bernard Robbins were two major influences on Bonime along with Erich Fromm who was part of the initial faculty of the new Institute (Bonime, 1989). As a result of my study with Bonime, I began to appreciate how faulty ways of interpersonal relating can result in painful ways of living that manifest in psychological symptoms. I learned that it is not possible to ignore the inner life of a person (the individual's memories of the past, feelings, thoughts, hopes, dreams, wishes, conflicts, and anxiety—the psychodynamics of the person), or the interpersonal, social and cultural context in which the person evolved. The idiosyncratic experiences of the person need to be pursued in great detail along with the unique context in which these experiences took place.

Another key tenet of the Culturalist Psychoanalytic approach is collaboration and partnership in the therapeutic process. Interpretations are offered in a tentative manner—inviting both analyst and client to consider it, modify it, reject it or build on it. Bonime viewed collaboration as essential to the therapeutic process. He explained, "Regardless of all therapeutic understanding, empathy, and skill, the essence of the total process of psychoanalysis is to engender and foster collaboration, the polar opposite of competitiveness. The development of a high degree of collaborative capacity, first achieved with the analyst, becomes, no matter what the patient's presenting difficulty, one of the most crucial gains in any successful psychoanalytic experience" (Bonime, 1989, p. 377).

Collaboration is a key principle underlying all the clinical work described in this book. A Native American Proverb (Ute) expresses this principle poetically, "Don't walk behind me, I may not lead. Don't walk in front of me; I may not follow. Walk beside me that we may be as one" (Zona, 1994. p. 57).

The wounds of contemporary youth can penetrate deep to their spirit, but the desire to heal also emanates from the depths of their soul. We should never minimize either the pain of the injuries or the resilient spirit of children as we assist them in their healing process. A nurse once told me that the strongest tissue in the body is scar tissue. In the chapters to follow the clinical illustrations will feature children who run the gamut from suffering anxiety and depression, common to contemporary life, to the stories of children who heroically survived some of the deepest wounds to the spirit. The stories will be told along with some of the theoretical and research background that guided the healing process. These are remarkable children who grew stronger in response to harsh early life experiences and are representative of many other children whose inspiring stories remain to be told. These children give new meaning to terms like strength, courage, determination, and resilience.

REFERENCES

American Psychological Association. (2007). *Report of the APA Task Force on the sexualization of girls.* Washington, DC: American Psychological Association.

Anderson R. N., & Smith, B. L. (2003). Deaths: Leading causes for 2001. *National Vital Statistics Report, 52,* 1–86.

Benedict, H. (2003). Object-relations/thematic play therapy. In Schaefer, C. (Ed.), *Foundations of play therapy* (pp. 281–305). New York: John Wiley.

Benedict, H. (2006). Object Relations Play Therapy: Applications to attachment problems and relational trauma. In C. E. Schaefer & H. G. Kaduson (Eds.), *Contemporary play therapy: Theory, research, and practice* (pp. 3–27). New York: Guilford Press.

Benedict, H., & Hastings, L. (2002). Object-relations play therapy. In F. W. Kaslow & J. J. Magnavita (Eds.), *Comprehensive handbook of psychotherapy: Psychodynamic/object relations, Vol. 1* (pp. 47–80). Hoboken, NJ: John Wiley & Sons.

Bonime, W. (1962). *The clinical use of dreams.* New York: Basic Books.

Bonime, W. (1989). *Collaborative psychoanalysis: Anxiety, depression, dreams, and personality change.* Rutherford, NJ: Fairleigh Dickinson University Press.

Bowlby, J. (1988). A secure base: *Parent-child attachment and healthy human development.* New York: Basic Books.

Cavoukian, R. & Olfman, S. (Eds.) (2006). *Child honoring: How to turn this world around.* Westport, CT: Praeger Publishers.

Currie, E. (2004). *The road to whatever: Middle-class culture and the crisis of adolescence.* New York: Metropolitan Books.

Curtis, R. C., & Hirsch, I. (2003). Relational approaches to psychoanalytic psychotherapy. In A. S. Gurman & S. B. Messer (Eds.), *Essential psychotherapies: Theory and practice* (2nd ed., pp. 69–106). New York: Guilford Press.

DeYoung, P. (2003). *Relational psychotherapy: A primer.* New York: Brunner-Routledge.

Friedman, T. L. 2006. *The world is flat: A brief history of the Twenty-first century* (Updated and expanded edition). New York: Farrar, Straus and Giroux.

Garbarino, J. (1995). *Raising children in socially toxic environments.* San Francisco: Jossey-Bass.

Garbarino, J. (1999). *Lost boys: Why our sons turn violent and how we can save them.* New York: Anchor Books, A Division of Random House.

Garbarino, J. (2006a). *See Jane hit: Why girls are growing more violent and what we can do about it.* New York: Penguin Press.

Garbarino, J. (2006b). *Words can hurt forever.* Daniel Kirk Memorial Lecture at Marist College, Poughkeepsie, NY. March 22.

Greenberg, L. (2004). Emotion-focused therapy. Presentation at the Psychotherapy Networker Symposium. Washington, DC.

Greenspan, S. I., & Shanker, S. G. (2006). The emotional architecture of the mind. In R. Cavoukian & S. Olfman (Eds.), *Child honoring: How to turn this world around* (pp. 5–15). Westport, CT: Praeger Publishers.

Haas-Cunningham, S. (in press). *The princess whose heart felt empty.* Unpublished manuscript. Syracuse, NY: Syracuse University.

Hardy, K. V. (2005). *Working with low-income families.* Presentation at the Ackerman Institute for the Family. New York.

Hardy, K. V., & Laszloffy, T. 2005. *Teens who hurt: Clinical interventions to break the cycle of adolescent violence.* New York: Guilford Press.

Hegel, G. F. W. (1979). *The phenomenology of spirit.* Translated by A. V. Miller. New York: Oxford University Press.

Hughes, D. A. (1997). *Facilitating developmental attachment: The road to emotional recovery and behavioral change in foster and adopted children.* Lanham, MD: Jason Aronson.

Hughes, D. A. (2006). *Building the bonds of attachment: Awakening love in deeply troubled children* (2nd ed.). Lanham, MD: Jason Aronson.

Hughes, D. A. (2007). *Attachment-focused family therapy.* New York: Norton.

Kasser, T. (2002). *The high price of materialism.* Cambridge, MA: MIT Press.

Lamb, S. (2006). *Sex, therapy, and kids: Addressing their concerns through talk and play.* New York: Norton.

Linn, S. (2006). Honoring children in dishonorable times: Reclaiming childhood from commercialized media culture. In R. Cavoukian & S. Olfman (Eds.), *Child honoring: How to turn this world around* (pp. 199–209).Westport, CT: Praeger Publishers.

Lukas, C. L. (2004). *Sex (Ms.) education: What young women need to know (but won't hear in women's studies) about sex, love and marriage.* Washington, DC: Independent Women's Forum. Retrieved May 24 2007, from http://www.iwf.org/pdf/sex_ms_ed1.pdf

Magnavita, J. J. (2006). In search of the unifying principles of psychotherapy: Conceptual, empirical, and clinical convergence. *American Psychologist, 61,* 882–92.

Marmot, M. G. (2006). Status syndrome: A challenge to medicine. *JAMA: Journal of the American Medical Association,* 295:1304–7.

McGee, Z. T., & Baker, S. R. (2002). Impact of violence on problem behavior among adolescents: Risk factors among an urban sample. *Journal of Contemporary Criminal Justice, 18,* 74–93.

McPherson, M., Brashears, M. E., & Smith-Lovin, L. (2006). Social isolation in America: Changes in core discussion networks over two decades. *American Sociological Review 71,* 353–75.

Miller, J. B. (1978). *Toward a new psychology of women.* Harmondsworth, England: Penguin.

Miller, J. B. (1986). *What do we mean by relationships?* Wellesley, MA: Stone Center for Developmental Services and Studies.

Miller, J. B., & Stiver, I. P. (1997). *The healing connection: How women form relationships in therapy and life.* Boston: Beacon Press.

Minuchin, S., & Fishman, H. C. (1981). *Family therapy techniques.* Cambridge, MA: Harvard University Press.

Minuchin, S., & Nichols, M. P. (1993). *Family healing: Tales of hope and renewal from family therapy.* New York: The Free Press.

Mitchell, S. A., & Aron, L. A. (Eds.). (1999). *Relational psychoanalysis: The emergence of a tradition.* Relational Perspectives Book Series, Vol. 14. Mahwah, NJ: Analytic Press.

O'Donohue, J. (2000). *Eternal echoes: Celtic reflections on our yearning to belong.* New York: HarperPerennial.

O'Sullivan, J. (2005). It's 420: Do you know where your children are? Adolescent substance use and misuse. *Clinical Excellence for Nurse Practitioners, 9,* 127–29.

Raskin, J. D. (2007). Assimilative integration in Constructivist Psychotherapy. *Journal of Psychotherapy Integration, 17,* 50–69.

Rokach, A. (2004). Loneliness then and now: Reflections on social and emotional alienation in everyday life. *Current Psychology: Developmental, Learning, Personality, Social, 23,* 24–40.

Ruchkin, V., Sukhodolsky, D. G., Vermeiren, R. Koposov, R., & Schwab-Stone. M. (2006). Depressive symptoms and associated psychopathology in urban adolescents: A cross-cultural study of three countries. *Journal of Nervous and Mental Disease, 194,* 106–13.

Schore, A. N. (1994). *Affect regulation and the origin of the self: The neurobiology of emotional development.* Hillsdale, NJ: Erlbaum.

Schore, A. N. (2003a). *Affect dysregulation and disorders of the self.* New York: Norton.

Schore, A. N. (2003b). *Affect regulation and the repair of the self.* New York: Norton.

Siegel, D. (1999). *The developing mind.* New York: Guilford Press.

Siegel, D. (2007). *The mindful brain: Reflection and attunement in the cultivation of well-being*. New York: Norton.

Silverstein, O. (1987). *The art of systems therapy*. A presentation at the Ackerman Institute for the Family. New York, NY.

U.S. Department of Health and Human Services, Administration on Children, Youth, and Families. (2005). *Child maltreatment 2003*. Washington, DC: Government Printing Office.

Waters, D. B. and E. C. Lawrence. (1993). *Competence, courage and change: An approach to family therapy*. New York: Norton.

Whybrow, P. C. (2005). *American mania: When more is not enough*. New York: Norton.

Zona, G. A. (1994). *The soul would have no rainbow and other Native American Proverbs*. New York: Touchstone Books.

2

Healing Wounds to the Spirit Camouflaged by Rage

Kenneth V. Hardy and David A. Crenshaw

OVERVIEW

When children and teens are hurting deeply within they often use various masks and disguises to hide the pain from both themselves and others. This chapter addresses the mask of aggressive, sometimes even violent acting-out behavior. While this is particularly common in boys, it is becoming more frequent among girls as well (Garbarino, 2006). The disguise, unfortunately, is quite effective and the inner pain stemming from the lacerations to their souls is often not recognized by others and they are ever so reluctant to acknowledge it themselves. Two such youth are discussed in this chapter to illustrate the key social, cultural, and intrapersonal dynamics along with key treatment issues.

RICK: TEEN DEPRESSION DISGUISED BY RAGE

The seventeen-year-old boy was non-communicative and glared at the therapist with venomous rage darting like laser beams from his eyes. Like most youth in trouble with the law or at school he experienced the mandate to attend therapy to be worst than going to a dentist for a root canal and only slightly better than going to jail. He was there because a judge ordered him to either attend therapy or go to jail after he had broken another student's jaw in a fight after a basketball game at his high school.

> Rick: I don't have any f _ _ _ing problems.
> Therapist: How then can we make this time together useful to you?
> Rick: How the f _ _ _ do I know? It is not my idea to come here.

Therapist: Whose idea was it?

Rick: The G _ d d _ _n judge.

Therapist: What work can we do together to satisfy the judge so you don't have to go to jail?

Rick: I already told you, I don't have any f _ _ _ing problems.

Therapist: Are you saying the judge will be satisfied when I with your consent send a report that explains, "Rick doesn't have any f _ _ _ing problems?"

Rick: F _ _ _ you. I hate this bull s _ _ t. I'd rather go to jail.

Therapist: You could make that choice. You could go back to court and let the judge know that you would rather go to jail than go to therapy. But as long as you're here, I would like to see if we can do something together that might be useful to you.

This is a brief sample of dialogue in the first session but it reveals the rough beginning of the work with Rick. Like many adolescents Rick had no trust in the system and only contempt for those he saw representing the system, teachers, school officials, judges, and therapists.

Rick's rage was never far below the surface ready to be triggered by the slightest provocation, real or imagined. The fight after the basketball game was one of numerous fights that had resulted in multiple school suspensions. The most serious prior incident occurred last school year when he took a swing at a teacher and was suspended for the remainder of the school year.

Teens Judged Harshly

Violence is deplorable and hideous. We do not condone it or excuse it. We have, however, come to know many kids like Rick and we strongly object to the ways these youths tend to be judged in a harsh and narrow, moralistic manner as simply "bad kids" and in need of harsher punishments and stiffer sentences. These punitive responses are typically futile because the core issues of unresolved major losses and often trauma are in no sense addressed by further punishment. We advocate for a more complex view of violent youth.

Embracing Complexity

Alan Kazdin, Director of the Yale Child Study Center, explained that youth aggression, like heart disease, does not have a single cause but rather results from a complex interaction of biological, genetic, social, and cultural contributions (Kazdin & Whitley, 2003). To simply blame these kids and their families is to fail to appreciate the complexity and to seize on a simplistic, reductionistic explanation. To embrace complexity is not the same as abdicating responsibility as parents, teens, teachers, schools, communities and societies. Violence in our youth is multi-determined but we are each accountable for our role. As parents, teachers, schools, communities, businesses and corporations, as societies, we need to step up to the plate. We need to be responsible for the environments, human contexts, and experiences we make available to our youth. Children, likewise, in developmentally appropriate ways need to be held accountable for the choices they make and the way they treat others.

It is hard to look past the ugliness of violence in all its forms to see the invisible, emotional wounds and all too frequently the profound losses and/or trauma that many violent teens have suffered. Not all violent youth grow up in poverty, violent homes or neighborhoods. Some grow up in affluent homes and neighborhoods but are emotionally impoverished and as James Garbarino (1999) has noted, "spiritually empty." They lack not only a sense of direction, but experience a deep void, a lack of meaning, or purpose to life. Genetic influences, temperament, even molecular or neurochemical factors may exert a primary influence in some cases of youth violence. In the latter case sociocultural factors may play a minor or extremely subtle role. If we appreciate complexity we will not attempt to pinpoint any single factor but rather explore what has caused the eruption of violence in this particular youngster in this specific family in this community at this point in time.

Rick's Hidden Wounds

Rick was a member of a working class family. He had a brother two years older who was attending a vocational school learning to be an auto mechanic. His brother had moved out a year ago to an apartment he shared with his girlfriend. His father had left four years earlier to move in with another woman whom he plans to marry. Since then Rick has had little contact with his father. The parents' divorce was legally finalized two years ago. Emotionally, however, it is not finished, not for Rick, and especially not for his mother.

When Rick's hostility didn't divert the therapist from pursuit of his underlying emotional pain the depression that was suggested by covert sadness in his first session became more pronounced and evident in later sessions. One day he confided to his therapist, "I feel like I carry a 140 lb. weight on my shoulders."

Therapist: That's an incredible amount of weight. What makes the load so heavy?
Rick: Things have worked out for my "ole man." He is probably happier than he has ever been, but not mom.

Therapist: What about your mom?

Rick: She is really depressed. She is drinking more than ever. She is really stressed out about paying her bills.

Therapist: You are really worried about your mom. What worries you the most?

Rick: She talks about suicide. When I come home from school I wonder what I am going to find.

Therapist: What goes through your mind when you come home from school?

Rick: My friend Mike and I walked in after school and found her passed out the floor. When I saw her lying on the floor I thought she was dead.

Therapist: No wonder that weight is so heavy; no wonder you feel like you are carrying 140 lbs on your back.

Rick: I never thought Mike would say anything but we were smoking weed in the parking lot before the basketball game and we both were getting high.

Therapist: That explains the fight—he said something at the basketball game about your mom?

Rick: I am not sorry I busted his jaw in two places. The bastard said in front of a lot of guys that my mom was a "falling down drunk."

Rick's act of violence was not justified. His rage, however, at the insult and humiliation in front of other students by a boy he considered to be his friend is understandable. It was one more blow to a teen who had already suffered major losses and assaults on his dignity. Perhaps no wound cuts more deeply than the betrayal of a once trusted friend.

When Rick with great courage took the harrowing risk of trusting his therapist enough to share his story and reveal the 140 lb. weight he was carrying, the therapist to Rick's great relief was able to commence work with his severely depressed/suicidal mother. Rick's violent actions could reasonably be viewed as a misguided attempt to get help for his mother about whom he was deeply distressed. He felt this load was his alone to shoulder after his father and then his brother moved out.

Unburdening

Over and over teens like Rick have taught us that if we persist in our determination to appreciate and respect their invisible wounds and recognize their devastating losses we eventually arrive at the inner chambers of their crushed hearts and souls. When they develop sufficient trust to unburden and tell their stories we learn of the heavy emotional loads they have carried. The emotional pain has in many instances been camouflaged by rage that eventually is triggered into episodes of violence. Their stories urgently need to be told and empathically heard. Adolescents resist telling their stories until absolutely convinced a trusted adult truly wants to hear it, but at the same time they have a strong urge to unburden their emotional pain. Alice Miller (1997) observed that when someone has experienced trauma he or she has a powerful need to have the pain witnessed by trusted others.

In Rick's case, the metaphor of the heavy weight proved useful throughout the course of therapy. At various points, the therapist would ask, "How heavy is that weight now?" Rick would answer, "I would say maybe about 80 lbs." The therapist responded, "That's still a lot of weight but nowhere near the 140 lbs. you were carrying before. Let's see if we can figure out a way to reduce the load further. Do you have some ideas?" A key feature of the work with angry, mistrusting adolescents is to engage them in a collaborative therapeutic process. Collaboration and mutual trust does not typically characterize their past experiences of relationships with adults. Respect for their ideas, feelings, and personhood is essential. Youth today receive so much correction but what they are often lacking is connection with the important adults in their lives (Hardy and Laszloffy, 2005). Due to repeated emotional injury, youth erect brick walls of anger, mistrust, and cynicism that seem at times impossible to penetrate. Yet, secretly they hope that we will succeed. As masterful as they are in discouraging us, they do not in the deeper recesses of their soul want to defeat us. The walls although protective, leave them lonely, despairing, and deprived of what makes life bearable—meaningful connections with others.

KAREEM: RAGE CAMOUFLAGING TRAUMATIC LOSS

His foster mother, Mrs. Gibson, an African American widow, adopted Kareem, also African American, when he was ten years old. He is now twelve years old. He has lived with his adoptive mother since age 5. Kareem's birth parents were alcohol and crack addicted and an off-duty policeman killed his father while in the process of robbing a convenience store. He has one sister Felicia who is two years younger and she also had been adopted by Mrs. Gibson. In addition, Mrs. Gibson has six other foster children living in her home ranging in age from 22 months to 18 years. Mrs. Gibson's husband died suddenly two years after Kareem and his sister were placed in the home.

There is much to consider when looking at Kareem's story from a multicultural perspective. He is twelve and an angry boy. He is an African American boy and there has been a significant legacy of loss in both his birth family and adoptive family. During the first five years of his life he endured extreme poverty and was exposed to violence and the nightmare of crack and alcohol addiction in both of his parents.

Mrs. Gibson reported that Kareem was often aggressive and verbally abusive toward family members. He had been hospitalized at a children's psychiatric center at age 8 for out of control, disruptive and violent behavior. A week after discharge from the hospital Kareem threatened his adoptive mother and sister with a butcher knife and he was re-hospitalized. Mrs. Gibson contacted the therapist (Crenshaw) after finding his name in the list of providers that took her insurance and we scheduled an initial consultation about Kareem.

Kareem came in with Mrs. Gibson and his sister, Felicia. He was sullen, angry and clearly uneasy about seeing still another therapist. Like so many children in the foster care system, Kareem had been seen at various times by a whole parade of mental health professionals trying to figure out what was wrong with him and he wanted nothing more to do with it. I honored his strategies of keeping distance. I told him that he had no reason to trust me because he had just met me and he has been through this process many times. I said, "I imagine that it is very hard for you to start over with still another person." I also told him that until he was convinced that I had something useful to offer him, I recommend that he stick with his plan of not letting me get too close. Mrs. Gibson expressed great concern that if something was not done that Kareem was going to hurt her and his sister or the foster children in the home.

Therapist: When did you start to be really worried about Kareem hurting you or his sister?

Mrs. Gibson: I don't know. I guess about 6–8 months ago it started to get really bad.

Therapist: Think about what was going on in the family about 6 to 8 months ago. Can any of you remember any changes that took place around that time?

Mrs. Gibson: Actually, come to think of it, that was in the spring, around the time that Michelle was placed in our home as a foster child.

Therapist: Michelle became your 6th foster child and altogether you now have 8 children in the home. What has that been like for you, Mrs. Gibson? How about for you, Kareem and Felicia? What is it like to be a part of such a large family?

Felicia: Michelle has caused a lot of trouble since she came. She is always starting fights. I can't stand the way she acts.

Mrs. Gibson: I think she is starting to calm down. She is only 9 and she has had a lot to get used to.

Kareem: (To Mrs. Gibson) You are always tired and bitchy. You are always on my case and it is not like it used to be.

Therapist: How did it used to be Kareem? How would you like it to be between you and your mother? Talk with her now about the changes you would like to see and how you feel it is not the same.

Kareem: I remember when you used to laugh more and tell funny stories and you had time to come to my basketball games, now you just drop me off and pick me up. You have no time to watch my games. I know you have been going to Dr. Bremer a lot lately. What's wrong?

Mrs. Gibson: I didn't know that you were worried about me. I am okay. I am just a little tired and have some problems with my blood pressure and I am trying a new medicine but it is nothing for you to worry about. It has been very crazy the last few months and I guess I haven't been in such a good mood. My husband died in the spring and it seems like every year I go through a tailspin around the time he was killed.

Therapist: How did your husband die?

Mrs. Gibson: In an accident at work. A beam fell off a crane at the construction site. It crushed him. It was horrible. It still is a shock. I can hardly believe it even now.

Therapist: How sad and heartbreaking—What a shock that must have been for all of you. The spring has multiple meanings for you, Mrs. Gibson, and your family. You added another member to your family at the very time you were emotionally re-experiencing the tragic and shocking loss of your husband. The needs of your own large family plus your need to attend to your grief has perhaps left Kareem feeling the loss of your availability to him—not only in terms of time but your ability to be there emotionally for him. Perhaps your ability to be there for Kareem has been temporarily diminished by your devastating sense of loss?

Kareem looked noticeably relieved as he realized it was not him that had caused his adoptive mother to withdraw. Rather she has been battling depression and has been deeply sad about the sudden death of her husband and also overwhelmed with the large brood of children for whom she is providing a home. He was also very glad to learn that his mother was not seriously ill—something that he had been worried about for the past 5 months due to the mother's frequent trips to the family physician.

Kareem's history of profound loss, his father's sudden death, the loss of both of his parents to drug and alcohol addiction, the sudden death of his adoptive father led him to react intensely to any shift in the family context. The adding of another foster child threatened his supplies of nurturance from his overwhelmed adoptive mother. The thought that she might be seriously ill was even scarier since she was the only parent that he and his sister have left. Her depression and emotional withdrawal felt to him like abandonment. Further he felt he was responsible for his mother's increased distance.

Repeated, Unacknowledged Losses

This is a story about a family that will be quite familiar to those who work in the foster care system and with children in out-of-home placements. The emotional underpinnings of aggressive acting-out behavior in boys so often point to a history of major losses. Furthermore, these losses are frequently unrecognized by others and may be either cognitively or emotionally unacknowledged by the child (Crenshaw and Hardy, 2005; Crenshaw and Garbarino, 2007; Crenshaw and Mordock, 2005a, 2005b; Hardy and Laszloffy, 2005). Kareem, for example, minimized the impact of his father's death by statements such as, "He was never around anyway" "I don't miss him—he was always smoking weed anyway." The affect is denied. This is a frequent pattern regarding father absence, especially with boys (Hardy and Laszloffy, 2005). Boys receive repeatedly the message that boys don't cry. "Get over it!" This invites a cut-off from their affective experience.

Support for the Adoptive Mother

In Kareem's family, the intervention was guided by the belief that his adoptive mother was feeling overwhelmed, depleted and depressed. It was clear that she had a long ways to go in working through her own grief over the traumatic death of her husband. Some individual sessions with her enabled her to talk in depth about her shock, anger, sorrow, loss of dreams and plans that she had shared with her husband.

While she and her husband had cared for foster children prior to his death she had never had more than four children in her home at one time. She now realizes her taking on the extra foster children, in addition to adopting Kareem and Felicia, was an attempt to busy herself with the care of the children so that she would not have time or opportunity to focus on her deep sorrow. She has now reached a point where she was emotionally depleted and the long avoided grief could no longer be denied.

The care of such a large family as a single mother had left her exhausted and it could not fill the void left by the unmourned death of her husband. As she shared more of her story and the underlying feelings that she had not wanted to face, her depression gradually began to lift. The therapist asked her what would be a realistic number of foster children for her to care for in her home, in addition to Kareem and Felicia. She decided that two foster children would be manageable and she made a plan with social services not to place anymore children to allow her to eventually get down to that number.

Individual Work with Kareem

Kareem needed individual time in therapy before working on strengthening his connections to his mother and sister. His story had always been one of insufficiency and feeling pushed aside. His sister was cute and more social than he. She was also doing better in school and was better behaved than him both at school and in the home. His biological parents were unavailable due to their drug addition, followed by the death of his father, and the surrendering of legal rights to her children by the mother. He had not heard anything about his birth mother following his placement in foster care. Like so many children in the foster care system, Kareem suffered from a series of unrecognized and acknowledged losses that were important for him to face and grieve.

Acknowledging the Losses

Serious consequences can result from losses that never receive the proper acknowledgment in keeping with the magnitude of the loss. As these losses accumulate, the child gradually loses his/her capacity to feel the pain of his/her own losses and ominously, also, loses the capacity to feel the pain of others. Loss becomes dehumanized and this is a central feature in the cycle of violence (Crenshaw and Hardy, 2005; Crenshaw and Garbarino, 2007; Garbarino, 1999; Hardy and Laszloffy, 2005).

At first, Kareem was very reluctant to discuss his birth parents and tried every diversionary tactic that he could think of. The therapist first worked on establishing a trusting and safe relationship with him. He was interested in the collection of dinosaurs and puppets in the office. Kareem, like many children we have known in foster care, was developmentally, emotionally and socially significantly younger than his chronological age. His play primarily focused on themes of aggression and rage with the dinosaurs and the aggressive puppets, alligator and crocodile, devouring the weaker and more vulnerable animals and puppet characters. Themes of loss were also prominent with death and destruction all around with some play characters disappearing and unable to be located.

Empathy with the Pain

Kareem also liked drawing and he did a number of spontaneous drawings of battle scenes reflecting, the chaos, conflict, and struggle that had characterized his life. Structured exercises were used to help him identify, label and express feelings in a picture series that requires the child to write in a cartoon bubble what he might feel in that situation. This allows for practice in the most important of all pro-social skills of being able to empathize with the feelings of others.

Therapist: Now can you tell me about a time when you felt just as scared, just as helpless; just as desperate as the man in the picture feels?

Kareem: When mom and dad got high and went crazy. One time my dad got into a fight over some money and the other man threatened to come back with a gun and shoot us all. I hid under my bed and was really scared.

Therapist: What was it like for you that your father died so suddenly in the way that he did?

Kareem: (a long pause) One night I woke up and I started crying so hard I thought I was going to wake everybody. I didn't know what it was about. It was kind of scary. I just felt like crying.

Therapist: Have there been other times when you felt very sad and felt like crying but you couldn't explain it?

Kareem: Sometimes I am mad at the whole world and I don't know why. That's when I get into trouble. My mom gets so fed up with me. I can't blame her, she has all those kids and I give her a hard time.

Therapist: Maybe you're angry not only because your birth parents weren't there for you, but Mrs. Gibson has a lot on her plate and although she means well perhaps you feel she can't be there for you either.

Kareem: Maybe.

Therapist: How about the death of your adoptive father? What was he like and how did you handle his sudden death?

Kareem: I don't like to talk about it. It really upsets Mom when she thinks about it. That was . . . I don't know. He was good to me and my sister. He laughed a lot and he liked to do things with us. He was only my Dad for I don't know—not long. I had two Dads die.

Therapist: I can't imagine what it would like to lose two Dads. I am sure it is very hard, you were just getting used to having a Dad who wanted to do things with you and then he gets killed too.

Kareem: Yeah.

Therapist: I am wondering how you made it through these really tough times. You and your sister had to manage a lot of time on your own when you were with your birth parents. What did you do when you were hungry or scared or lonely to get through those times?

Kareem: The places that we lived were mostly pretty dangerous, very scary, but there usually was somebody in the neighborhood that I knew we could go to if something happened.

Therapist: If we pretended that I was a talk show host and I had you on my TV program as an expert in survival under tough conditions what would you want to tell the boys and girls listening to our program about how to cope when things are really bad?

Kareem: That's a tough one.

Therapist: But you know a lot about what it takes. You've been there and you have survived. What helped you get through it all?

Kareem: I guess I knew I had to for my sister. She was so little, so scared. She used to cry a lot. I would try to make funny faces or do silly things to get her mind off of being scared. It sometimes worked, but sometimes she would just cry. I always thought that someday things would get better.

HOPE AND SURVIVAL

This therapeutic exchange points to the crucial difference that hope can play in helping children as well as adults survive under harsh life circumstances. How Kareem was able to retain hope under the conditions that he and his sister lived is a testament to the incredible resilience of the human spirit. We are in awe of youngsters like Kareem who have provided a lifetime's worth of inspiration to us.

DISCONNECTION FROM AFFECT

The dialogue above also points to the disconnection between cognitive awareness and the underlying painful affect (Kareem woke up sobbing but he didn't know why; he had periods of extreme anger at the whole world that he couldn't explain). Also the tendency to deny and minimize the loss that is especially typical of boys in our culture (Hardy, 2003) was evident when I inquired about his father's death ("I don't think about him").

> Kareem: I don't know. I don't think of him as a Dad. He was never in my life the way other kids' Dads are. I don't really think about him.
>
> Therapist: Only you can say what it is like for you. But sometimes when kids tell me that, I don't buy it completely. They will tell me, "My Dad was never around, and he never had time with me so I don't really miss him." In a way I know they are correct. It is hard to miss someone who never was a part of your life. But I often find with the kids who tell me that—in their quiet and alone moments there is some sadness, they feel a loss. Maybe, it is for something they had hoped for and wished for from a Dad that they now know will never happen. Do you ever in your quiet and alone moments have feelings like that?
>
> Kareem: Maybe I do. Sometimes I feel sad but I don't know why.

Grieving the Loss of Dreams

Kareem was asked to do some drawings that were focused on favorite memories. None of the pictures contained his birth parents but there were pictures of school and family outings that took place after coming to live with Mrs. Gibson. I then asked him to draw a picture of what he would have liked his early life to be. He drew a picture of two parents, a boy and a girl at a park. The mother and daughter were setting out food at a picnic table. The father and son were sitting side by side and fishing in a small lake nearby. I then asked him to draw a picture of how his life really was like. Kareem drew a picture of him and his sister playing in the street.

Therapist: How old are you and your sister in the picture?

Kareem: I guess I am about four and she is about two.

Therapist: Where are your parents while you're playing in the neighborhood?

Kareem: I don't know.

Therapist: Do you remember other times when you and your sister were alone and you didn't know where your parents were?

Kareem: Lots of times?

Therapist: What was that like for you?

Kareem: Sometimes really scary. It was not a safe place. It was very scary.

Therapist: You were very young to be looking after your two-year-old sister. Did anyone notice that you were looking after your sister and her parents were not around?

Kareem: Yeah, that's when we went to our foster home.

Therapist: Can you remember a time before coming to Mrs. Gibson when you felt especially sad and lonely?

Kareem: Lots of times when we were in the apartment alone.

Therapist: You and your sister have been through a lot together. It is good that you have been able to stick together.

Kareem: I am mean to her sometimes. But I look out for her.

Therapist: You had to be strong and look out for her when you were only a little boy yourself. But you did it. Even though you sometimes can be rough on your sister you also have been a good big brother who looked out for her when there was no one else to do it. She is lucky to have a big brother like you. Who looks out for the two of you now?

Kareem: My mom.

Therapist: I can see why you were so worried when you thought she might be ill. She is very important to you.

Kareem: You can say that again.

Anger, Rage and Sorrow

Since the underlying rage and sorrow in this youngster was profound but hard to access in the therapeutic context, he was asked to show how angry he sometimes feels inside when he thinks about his life and some of the really hard things he faced. Since he was perplexed how to express this, I asked him if he could draw a picture of a volcano that would reveal how angry he feels when it is most intense (Crenshaw and Mordock, 2005a).

Therapist: Can you tell me about your picture?

Kareem: Nothing but red-hot lava spilling all over the place.

Therapist: Can you tell me who the "I hate you!" and "F_ _ _ you!" is intended for?

Kareem: Sometimes everybody, the whole world.

Therapist: You feel sometimes that the whole world has screwed you over?

Kareem: I sure as hell do.

Therapist: You know I would probably feel the same way if I had suffered as many losses as you! I would probably want to scream "I hate you" and "F_ _ _ you" too. How about the other times when you are feeling red-hot overflowing anger? Is there anyone in particular you are furious with?

Kareem: How could parents not care about their kids? I hate Mom and Dad for what they did. Sometimes I wish I could have a meeting with my mother (birth mother) and tell her off.

Therapist: What would you like to say to her?

Kareem: Listen you bitch. You ruined your life, my life, and my sister's. What was wrong with you? The drugs were a lot important than your children to you. I hope you rot in hell.

Therapist: You have every reason for being as angry as you are. One place that I see it differently is that the ruining your life part is going to be up to you. You and your sister were cheated out of a good beginning in life. You never had the security, love, protection and care that a child needs for a good start. I am not going to pretend that it will be easy but it is possible with even a bad start that your life need not be ruined. You no longer have to go it alone. There are people in your life now who care about you and are there to help you. In fact, why don't we take a moment to do something together? Let's trace either your hand or mine on this sheet of paper. Which one shall we do?

Kareem: Let me do yours.

Therapist: Okay. Now I want you to write on each finger and the thumb the name of someone, five people all together, who care about you and are here to help you.

Kareem proceeded to write on the "Helping Hand" (Strauss, 1999) fingers, his mom, his sister, two of his friends, and his therapist. Kareem was no longer alone in the world although he faced an uphill struggle and a long, rough road to traverse. It is essential that therapists not become overwhelmed with their own sense of hopelessness if they are going to be able to offer hope to these young people going against the odds.

Providing the Tools to Facilitate Affect Recognition and Expression

There is significant healing potential in dialogue (Bonime, 1989; Hardy and Laszloffy, 2005). The dialogue with Kareem, although just the beginning of the therapeutic discourse, illustrates that children are able to communicate about their affective experience when we structure the communication and make it easier for them to respond. Since children have a limited capacity to describe and delineate their feeling states we need to give them tools that facilitates their ability to share their inner world. Specific strategies to facilitate dialogue about grief and loss can be found in previous writing (Crenshaw, 2005, 2006, 2007; Crenshaw and Mordock, 2005a). Children who are particularly unable to verbalize may still be able to express themselves through artwork and dramatic play with puppets or animals.

Final Phase: Restoring Connections

The final phase of the therapeutic work with Kareem focused on restoring the emotional connection with his mother and sister. At times the three of them were seen together, and at other times, Kareem with his mother or Kareem with his sister. The goal was to strengthen the attachments through shared grief, disappointment, and loss and to share the unexpressed resentments that had led to distance and detachment. The good times together were punctuated and they planned ways to create happy memories together for the future. Mrs. Gibson was very convincing in expressing to both Kareem and Felicia that they were very important to her and that she was going to do her best to be more emotionally available to them.

Respect for the Emotional Wounds

Kareem was a child suffering invisible wounds of abandonment, loss, rejection, devaluation, shame and rage. It would be unfair to judge him based narrowly on his acting-out behavior. Under the aggression a deeply wounded, lonely and sad child resided who never before was able to grieve. If respect and acknowledgment of the invisible emotional wounds is not offered the profound losses of these children go unrecognized (Garbarino, 1999; Hardy and Laszloffy, 2005). The time to grieve may sadly never come for many youth similar to Kareem who are left to struggle alone with their unrecognized profound sorrow.

While the causes of youth violence span the landscape of a wide range of contributing influences and no one factor can explain it, we can't help but wonder how many youth who eventually commit a hideous violent act have compelling stories that need to be told, who carry heavy emotional burdens that need to be lifted or shared with others, who have suffered repeated losses never grieved, and who bear the scars from wounds of devaluation and oppression that need to be attended to so the healing process can begin. We can't help but wonder if their stories had been told to an empathic healer whether the deplorable acts of violence might have been averted. We wonder.

REFERENCES

Bonime, W. (1989). *Collaborative psychoanalysis: Anxiety, depression, dreams, and personality change.* Rutherford, NJ: Fairleigh Dickinson University Press.

Crenshaw, D. A. (2005). Clinical tools to facilitate treatment of childhood traumatic grief. *Omega: Journal of Death & Dying, 51,* 239–55.

Crenshaw, D. A. (2006). *Evocative strategies in child and adolescent psychotherapy.* Lanham, MD: Rowman & Littlefield Publishers.

Crenshaw, D. A. (2007). An interpersonal neurobiological-informed treatment model for childhood traumatic grief. *Omega, 54,* 315–32.

Crenshaw, D. A., & Garbarino, J. (2007). The hidden dimensions: Profound sorrow and buried human potential in violent youth. *Journal of Humanistic Psychology, 47,* 160–74.

Crenshaw, D. A., & Hardy, K. V. (2005). Understanding and treating the aggression of traumatized children in out-of-home care. In N. Boyd-Webb Press (Ed.), *Working with traumatized youth in child welfare* (pp.171–95). New York: Guilford.

Crenshaw, D. A., & Mordock, J. M. (2005a). *A handbook of play therapy with aggressive children.* Lanham, MD: Rowman & Littlefield Publishers.

Crenshaw D. A., & Mordock, J. M. (2005b). *Understanding and treating the aggression of children: Fawns in gorilla suits.* Lanham, MD: Rowman & Littlefield Publishers.

Garbarino, J. (1999). *Lost boys: Why our sons turn violent and how we can save them.* New York: Anchor Books, A Division of Random House.

Garbarino, J. (2006). *See Jane hit: Why girls are growing more violent and what we can do about it.* New York: Penguin Press.

Hardy, K. V. (2003). *Working with aggressive and violent youth.* Presentation at the Psychotherapy Networker Symposium. Washington, DC.

Hardy, K. V., & Laszloffy, T. (2005). *Teens who hurt: Clinical interventions to break the cycle of adolescent violence.* New York: Guilford Press.

Kazdin, A. E., & Whitley, M. K. (2003). Treatment of parental stress to enhance therapeutic change among children referred for aggressive and antisocial behavior. *Journal of Consulting and Clinical Psychology, 71,* 504–15.

Miller, A. (1997). *The drama of the gifted child.* New York: Basic Books.

Straus, M. B. (1999). *No-Talk therapy for children and adolescents.* New York: Norton.

3

Healing the Wounds of Children in a Family Context

Andrew Fussner and David A. Crenshaw

OVERVIEW

Partnership with families can greatly aid the healing process. The resources of the family facilitate healing when they are enlisted in a collaborative way. Families as imperfect as they may be potentially offer the safe harbor that all children need in their developmental years and that even as adults we return to for comfort and solace. Sadly, they can also be the source of indescribable destructiveness.

The wounding of the child's core self does not take place in a vacuum but in a human context. Likewise healing must take place in a human context and is particularly effective within the structure of the child's family. Salvador Minuchin in a consultation to the Astor Home for Children in October of 1994 observed that the art of family therapy was making the family responsible for healing without blaming them for the problem. This is a delicate but critical operation that mostly rests on the mindset of the therapist. We will never heal families if our mindset is to blame them whether that attitude is conveyed overtly or in quite subtle, covert form. The families will read the attitude of the therapist either way.

The meaning of the word "family" is different in family therapy now than it was in the early years. Family therapy theoreticians and practitioners have grown beyond the image of one man and one woman married to each other, having children, and raising them as partners. Indeed, the majority of families with children in the United States are single parent or three generational female-headed structures. There exist also a growing number of families in which children live with grandparents or with two same sex parents. The family therapist looks at the affective quality in these contexts regardless of the age, gender, sexual orientation or marital status of the parental figures.

THE ART OF SYSTEMS THERAPY

Symptoms as Metaphors

In family systems theory the symptom is not to be believed in and of itself. The symptom has to do with the structure and quality of the attachments in the child's relational context. The specific symptom has metaphorical significance, and should be understood as a message emanating from the interpersonal context not from an individual child. The clinician appreciates that the younger the child the more likely the symptom(s) will reflect the exact affective state of an important caregiver in the child's life. A three-year-old child has very little emotional influence outside the immediate circle of the primary caregivers, and therefore the clinician can confidently inquire about the emotional state of those caregivers. The emotional field around a seven-year-old child is greater than that of a three year old, the field around a child of eleven widens further, as it does even more for a child of fourteen, etc.

The affective significance of aggressive symptoms, for example, often reflects the longing for connection, and wish for proximity with one of the significant persons in the child's life. The more aggressive they are, the more they feel cut-off. No one has touched the child's heart in a long time. No one has recently tuned into the inner life of the child. It is frequent that acts of aggression from a child are covering up the stronger feelings of sadness or depression.

If the child is depressed, the family therapist is curious about whether anyone else in the child's circle of family and important attachments is depressed. If the child is excessively powerful or out of control, the family systems therapist will explore the hierarchical structure in the family. Who is elevating her? Who is inflating her power? Is the child being used as an instrument in an unspoken power struggle between the parental figures? There may be intensely conflictual issues that are too volatile to bring into the open for the family. The struggle gets detoured through the child.

If the child is running away—the family therapist becomes curious about from what or from whom is the child escaping or if there is anyone else in the family who secretly wants to make a run for it. The age of the child is important to consider in running away behavior. Younger children are almost invariably escaping from a dangerous or overwhelming situation. If the child has an uncontrollable temper—the family therapist wants to know who else in the family is prone to be violent. Violent or physically aggressive behaviors can be interpreted as efforts on the part of the child to reenact a scenario that he/she has witnessed in the family context. "Who hits, punches, kicks in your home when they get mad?" is a useful question to begin to expand the understanding of the symptom.

Anxiety in a child can be indicative of the presence of anxiety in one of the important figures in the child's life. This is particularly well demonstrated in cases of separation anxiety where the child appears to be frightened to leave home, or go to school, or to socialize with peers. An important figure in the child's life is frightened of separating from the child because of a separation trauma that occurred in the past of the parental figure or the possibility of danger in the present. If sibling rivalry is chronic and unusually intense, it is often a reflection of the anxiety of the children. They have a need to get the parents to focus on the sibling fight rather than fighting with each other or perhaps the parent(s) going out to use drugs. These are all hypotheses that may or may not pertain to a particular family but these possibilities need to be kept in mind by the family therapist.

The Significance of the Timing of Symptoms

A matter of great curiosity is the timing of the symptom. When it first appeared, what other events were going on in the family's life? These are important questions to ask not only for the information, but also to stimulate the curiosity of the family about these key issues. Peggy Papp (1983) stated, "The occurrence of a symptom may be precipitated by a multitude of events. It may be triggered by a change in one of the larger systems in which the family exists, such as the social, political, cultural, or educational system. For example: an economic depression resulting in unemployment or disastrous financial losses; a political crisis that tears the family apart, either physically or ideologically; a social revolution, such as occurred during the 1960s, that overturns conventions and rigid roles; poor educational methods or facilities; and racial, social, or sexual discrimination. All are part of wider cybernetic circuits that affect those of the family. Or, the precipitating event may come from inside the family as a reaction to some life cycle occurrence, such as the death of a grandparent, the birth of a child, a debilitating illness, or the departure of children from home" (pp. 9–10).

In previous writing (Crenshaw, 1990, 2005) these precipitating events were identified as "final straws." The final straw may be a subsequent loss that brings into focus earlier unresolved losses, such as a death, divorce, an abortion or a life transition. The life transition may include pregnancy, relocation, or perhaps a developmental step, such as graduation from college. Whatever the precipitating event may be it resonates with the earlier unresolved losses.

Reframing the Presenting Problem as Relational

The pioneering work of Salvador Minuchin in Structural Family Therapy has informed our work with families of children with wounded hearts along with many others, especially Olga Silverstein. Silverstein (1987) explained that she always set the context for the family work from the outset. She reframed the presenting problem so that it is *relational*; it is *purposeful*; it is something that they can have some *control over.*

Change/Stability Balance

Among other seminal family therapists, Silverstein (1987) pointed out the paradox that when families come to therapy they essentially say, "Change me, but make sure things stay the same." She paid close attention to what she called the *change-stability balance* and focused intensely on the *negative consequences of change.*

A major tenet of the systemic paradigm is that if the symptomatic behavior is what stabilizes the relationships in the family, the family will be destabilized if the therapy leads to change. Silverstein would sometimes restrain change by saying to a family, "Let's rehearse how to get things back to the way they were in case you want to" (1987). She pointed out that all change has both positive and negative consequences. These consequences are made explicit so the family can make an informed choice.

One common negative consequence of change is that if the presenting problem stops being a problem, what other problems in the family will become more visible? How will that affect the family? Who in the family might be most affected if the other problems are focused on? Silverstein observed that frequently in family therapy we learn what was valued in the original family is dysfunctional in the family of marriage.

Cut-Offs and Estrangement

In the families of children with injuries to the spirit it is important to look at the heart to heart connections within the family. Often what you will see are disconnections or cut-offs. Rage is often rooted in the pain of the sense of emptiness and deprivation of meaningful connection with attachment figures. It is very important to observe who is connected to whom and who is isolated within the family. Disconnection is often the source of unbearable psychic pain and one of the primary reasons for disturbances in affect and behavioral regulation.

Olga Silverstein gave a presentation (March 10, 1995) at the Ackerman Institute for the Family in New York titled, "Inclusion/Exclusion." She explained that American culture is dedicated to individuality with independence being the hallmark of maturation. In matrimony she observed, "You cleave to each other forsaking all others." Silverstein further noted that cutting off from family of origin was important as a consequence of the industrial revolution when young people left farms and villages to go to the cities for work. In contrast to the cultural ideal of cutting off and disconnecting from family of origin with independence viewed as the highest achievement of maturation, Silverstein believe that anytime family therapists can open up and expand the connections you will benefit the family.

In the 1970s and 1980s, Silverstein explained, a principal goal of therapy was helping children separate from their parents, to individuate. Our goal, rather according to Silverstein, should be inclusion. She observed that our culture has deprived us of what makes life endurable, which is a connection to others. A connection to family, friends, and community is vitally important. Furthermore, the pain of disconnection can be harder to deal with than death because it is a more confusing loss. Often there is a sense of loss that comes with disconnection that drives the acting-out behavior of the children. In these families it becomes important to help them grieve the pain of loss and disconnection. In adolescents the intensity of the acting out tends to diminish as they are able to express their sorrow in tears and words. The work becomes emotionally focused helping the family to express their long buried grief.

In families, when there is estrangement and alienation between the parent(s) and the child, it may be that the child reminds the parent(s) of some trauma in their past life. Perhaps the child was conceived under traumatic circumstances or born at a time when a relationship broke off or someone died. If this kind of issue is lurking in the shadows it can be crazy making for the child.

It is important to bring these issues out in the open and address them because it is no secret to the child that there is a cut-off with the parent(s) but the reasons are mysterious. If they know the truth as painful as it may be, they are in a better position to cope with it rather than relying on only their fantasies and imagination to fill in the gaps.

The Good Grief program (Trozzi and Massimini, 1999) in Boston has a slogan that "Unmentionable is unmanageable." No matter how horrible the reality, children can deal with a known situation better than an imagined one; a situation that can't be talked about with the adults in the child's life.

Developmental Markers

In observing families you might notice that a nine year-old child is being treated like he was six. Or a child of fifteen is behaving and being treated as a ten year old. The therapist becomes curious about the developmental history of the family. If the parents are treating the child as a much younger child—the family therapist will want to explore the hypothesis that the family is stuck in the past. Could there have been an emotional trauma in the life of a parent or the family that occurred around the time the child was six? A child whose symptomatic presentation indicates a delay in development often coincides with an unresolved traumatic event from the family's past. If the child were treated as if she is much older than her chronological age, we would wonder whether the parents are pushing her out the door. Are the parents overwhelmed? Are they burnt out from parenting? Are they unable to tolerate the dependency of their child? Are they in a big hurry to move on to the next chapter of their life? Does that entail a significant change in the life of the family? Could there be a secret plan to leave a spouse when the child is grown? In situations where the child is socially, emotionally, or sexually too advanced for her years it is useful to explore possible stressors in the current life of the family which may be intolerable.

Parents often need assistance in learning to accommodate the growth and development of their children. Inflexible family systems are a recipe for trouble especially when kids reach adolescence. Minuchin and Fishman (1981) explained, "As the child grows and her needs change, the parental subsystem must change as well. As the child's capacity increases, she must be given more opportunities for decision making and self-control. Families with adolescent children should negotiate differently from families with younger children. Parents with older children should give more authority to the children while demanding more responsibility from them" (p. 18).

The Emotional Space within the Parental Dyad

Another hypothesis to consider is whether the disturbance in the child is an expression of unresolved or unexpressed but powerful affect in or between parental figures. Children take in and react to the emotional process of the family particularly the emotional interplay between the parents. If the emotional space between the parents is toxic, symptoms are likely in one or more of the children. The behavioral disturbance in the child thus reflects the turbulence in the space between the parents. If the child is suicidal, it is important to pursue whether one or both parents are entertaining suicidal thoughts. If the child is out of control, perhaps one or both parents are out of control? If these hunches are correct, you can rest assured that the children will be worried and anxious each day as to whether one or both parents will leave, is the father going to beat up his mother, or is somebody going to commit suicide?

It has always been striking to us how much children worry about their parents and parents are often shocked when children with the encouragement of the family therapist are able to talk to them about these worries. Often, the parent(s) will say, "I had no idea that he was worried about me (us)."

Empowering Families

It is important to help family members realize the choices they made in their lives and take responsibility for them-to realize that they do have choices. How were the choices made? On what grounds were they made? Why were those choices made at that particular time? They are not powerless (Silverstein, 1995).

Structural family therapy is about empowering not invalidating parents. Braulio Montalvo, one of Salvador Minuchin's earliest colleagues, recalls a time when he was working with a mother and her four out-of-control children (Wylie, 2005). The mother felt overwhelmed, inadequate, and defeated in dealing with her children. One day while Minuchin and the mother were watching behind a one-way mirror, Montalvo took the four children into the therapy room to try to create some structure and order among these disruptive children and by his own account dramatically failed. Minuchin used the opportunity to point out that her kids were indeed hard to handle and it wasn't just her inadequacy. In fact, watching how the therapist struggled made her feel more competent (Wylie, 2005).

Families often enter into therapy with feelings of failure and incompetence. The embarrassment that their child has a symptom eclipses all the natural resources that likely are present in each of the family members. The therapist seeks to highlight those resources.

Cultural influences can militate against parents taking effective leadership even though children look to their parents to take charge. Minuchin and Fishman (1981) stated, "In our child-oriented culture, we tend to stress the obligations of the parents and pay less attention to their rights. But the subsystem that is given tasks must also have the authority to carry them out. And although a child must have the freedom to explore and grow, she will feel safe to explore only if she has the sense that her world is predictable" (p. 19).

Empowerment of families has been a time-honored goal of family therapy. Minuchin and Nichols (1993) observed, "The basic quest of family therapy is to release unused possibilities. That is the basis of its optimism. Families organize their members into certain patterns and, to an extent, it could not be otherwise. In order to feel secure, people must be part of predictable interactions. Unfortunately, predictability may congeal into limiting molds, so that the patterns become inflexible and family members use only a small range of the behaviors available to them" (Minuchin and Nichols, 1993, p. 45).

THE MYRIAD MANIFESTATIONS OF WOUNDED FAMILIES

Inability to See Danger

Most parents do their best to protect their children, but those with severe abuse histories of their own are often unable to appreciate or see the danger their children are placed in. Therefore, they are not able to adequately protect them from potential abusers. To see the danger would be tantamount to having to confront their own painful history of abuse and they may be emotionally unprepared to do so. This is often a most delicate time for the family therapist. The unresolved experiences of the parental figure are crucial to bringing about change in the child's behavior and state of mind. The engagement of the family therapist was initiated because of a current symptom in the child yet the therapist perceives the historical roots of the problem. There must be a strong bond between the therapist and parental figure before opening the door to the past. The shadows of the past linger long and dark in the clinical scenario, and most often these shadows are not in the awareness of the family.

A classic paper is "Ghosts in the Nursery" (Fraiberg, Adelson, and Shapiro, 1975). The authors explained, "In every nursery there are ghosts. They are the visitors from the unremembered past of the parents; the uninvited guests at the christening. Under all favorable circumstances the unfriendly and unbidden spirits are banished from the nursery and return to their own subterranean dwelling place. The baby makes his own imperative claim upon parental love and, in strict analogy with the fairy tales; the bonds of love protect the child and his parents against the intruders, the malevolent ghosts" (p. 387). Fraiberg and associates further elaborate, "The key to our ghost story appears to lie in the fate of affects in childhood. Our hypothesis is that access to childhood pain becomes a powerful deterrent against repetition in parenting, while repression and isolation of painful affect provide the psychological requirements for identification with the betrayers and the aggressors" (1975, p. 420). These authors provided a powerful testament to the heart of healing a family when they concluded, "In each case, when our therapy has brought the parent to remember and reexperience his childhood anxiety and suffering, the ghosts depart, and the afflicted parents become the protectors of their children against the repetition of their own conflicted past" (1975, pp. 420–21).

Blurred Boundaries

Healthy boundaries in a family are crucial to the development of children. In some families of wounded children the parents may be unable to exercise executive leadership. They need coaching and support to provide direction to their children. They may not be able to set limits or they may spend endless hours in futile arguments or debating with their children, but no clear direction is given. The children are at sea since they lack reliable internal controls and the external structure is inconsistent and shaky. Parentification is typical and frequently necessary in single parent families. The distribution of roles and responsibilities is different and healthy in these families. When the parent is overwhelmed, lonely and enjoys little life of his or her own the parentified child is more likely to develop a symptom. James Garbarino (1999) discussed the kind of role reversal common in the lives of violent boys where the child is the protector and the parent is needy. He observed that once this pattern is established it becomes extremely difficult for the parent to assert leadership particularly when the boys reached adolescence. Garbarino noted, "They may seek to discipline or exert control, but it is usually futile, because once he has been his mother's protector, he is not about to see her as an authority figure" (1999, p. 56).

In some of these families substance abuse or major psychiatric disorder is a major factor. Often the parent is depleted, the needle is on empty, and there is no more gas in the tank. In these situations the child gets pulled into a care-giving role with the parent and younger siblings. The crucial issues to be addressed are: "Who cares for the parent? Who is in his or her corner?" If no one is caring for the parent it is going to be hard for the parent to care for the child. The parent has no caring context.

Children in blended families have a more complicated system to negotiate and boundaries can be particularly fluid and blurred in such systems. Minuchin (1984) stated, "Children in blended families are often operating in a much more complex field than their parents. They may be active participants of two family systems, sometimes shuttling between two households, or at least maintaining contact with the remnants of the old family system and whatever additional membership that group has developed. If the new spouses push the children to accommodate to the new family, rather than permit them to evolve a complex solution to a complex problem, the children may well respond by 'freezing in place.' Put another way, to the extent that the parents are asking them to negate the past, they will refuse to accept the present" (pp. 68–69).

Monica McGoldrick in a presentation (1998) titled "Making Remarried Families Work" at the Family Therapy Networker Symposium estimated that half of all children born today will spend some portion of their growing up in a remarried family. McGoldrick described the complicated loyalty issues and ambiguities but recommended that intervention should be aimed in all but extreme cases involving danger or harm to the child to recognize that the child needs access to all the relevant people in his life. McGoldrick emphasized that these families have to tolerate ambiguity of losses, "the dangling ends." The loyalties and losses associated with the previous ties have to be recognized. Parents need to have respect for biological bonds and make space for the loyalties and attachments that exist.

McGoldrick (1998) also emphasized the importance of validating the loss the child feels when a parent remarries. Single parents tend to have more intimate relationships with their children. When the parent remarries they feel a real loss. Often when the parent remarries the contact between the children and the other biological parent lessens creating a double loss for the child. Children also experience a tremendous loss of the social network that existed prior to the divorce. This is especially true if they were required to move, change communities and schools. McGoldrick stated strongly that it should never be the children's responsibility to decide who they are going to live with.

Betrayals, Reconciliation, and Forgiveness—Lesions of the Heart

When rage in children reaches homicidal proportions, frequently there has been a major betrayal within the family. Evan Imber-Black and Peggy Papp, from the Ackerman Institute for the Family, discussed this issue in a presentation (2000) on "Betrayals and Reconciliation" at the Psychotherapy Networker Symposium. When family feuds or betrayals occur and they are not unusual in families seen in clinical settings, they typically cause deep emotional lacerations. Trust is lost and communication and negotiation seem impossible. Such feuds and betrayals can lead to permanent cut-offs in families. Imber-Black and Papp observed that usually a final straw occurs after cumulative hurt, followed by a desire to get revenge.

Revenge is a powerful tool that people are reluctant to give up. Often in the cases of children, the betrayal takes the form of abuse or witnessing domestic violence. It is tragic when hatred, grudges, and revenge splinter families, and in extreme cases, preclude reconciliation. We have known families where such divisions were maintained throughout life and carried to their graves. Imber-Black and Papp identified the following three key elements of reconciliation:

1) Acknowledgment of the hurt caused
2) The apology needs to be given wholeheartedly without qualification
3) Acceptance by the injured party

Imber-Black and Papp pointed out that asking "why" is a dead-end. The important thing is that the offending party accepts complete responsibility. There always must be a promise for something different in the future and a follow through in actions. They suggested that the therapist must set limits on blaming, name-calling and accusations.

Imber-Black and Papp (2000) pointed out that what is forgivable and un-forgivable depends on familial, religious and cultural background. Even if they can't forgive, it doesn't mean that they have to cut-off. We have observed devastating pain in families caused by cut-offs. As a way of trying to open up new possibilities, the Ackerman group suggested that the therapist ask solution and future oriented questions such as, "If you could find a solution what do you imagine it would be like?" "In your experience, how do people bridge such a gap?" "What small steps can help to bridge the distance?" They will point out to the family, "You may not be able to forget, but you can choose what to do about it when you remember" (Imber-Black and Papp, 2000).

Family splits, feuds, cut-offs, and betrayals are often at the heart of the anguish in families. Other questions that can be asked in these situations are: "What would it take for you to bury the hatchet?" "What is the legacy you want to leave your children or grandchildren?" "Will it serve you best to hold this grudge and carry it in your heart or to let it go?" "What would you have to give up in order to forgive?" "We have been trying to figure out whose heart is breaking the most, you who have offended or you who have been offended?" We often will add, "It must cause great pain to the heart to have hurt badly someone you once loved and it must be unbelievably painful not to be able to forgive someone you once loved dearly."

Psychosomatic Families—The Wounds Are Internalized

Children with wounded hearts sometimes externalize their pain by act-ing-out in aggressive or destructive ways while others internalize their pain, become depressed and/or engage in self-harming behaviors including eating disorders. The pain of the family tends to be expressed through the medium of somatic symptoms within a child. In some families the children may manifest various physiological symptoms such as stomachaches and gastrointestinal symptoms of various kinds, headaches, and frequent minor illnesses. Clearly, the first step is for the children to see their pediatrician to rule out any medical causes. Minuchin, Rosman, and Baker (1978) explained typical family dynamics, "Many psychosomatic families deny the existence of any problems whatsoever, see 'no need' ever to disagree, and are highly invested in consensus and harmony. Other psychosomatic families disagree openly, but constant interruptions and subject changes obfuscate any conflictual issue before it is brought to salience. Family members quickly mobilize to maintain a manageable threshold of conflict" (p. 32).

Children who develop eating disorders often are entangled in a web typical of enmeshed families. In these families, children often experience their parents as smothering and intrusive. In family therapy one of the key goals is to establish boundaries and ensure that each family member has a distinct voice. "The parents in an anorectic family typically intervene in arguments among the children, often to protect the anorectic child. Such intervention allies the anorectic inappropriately with her parents and robs her of the opportunity to participate in peer negotiations as an equal. The therapist must create a buffer zone, delineating the sibling subsystem" (Minuchin, Rosman, and Baker, 1978, p. 100). Frequently both parents are extremely overprotective of the anorectic. Sometimes the family therapist can assist in freeing the symptomatic child who is the focus of parental overprotectiveness and excessive, if not intrusive concern, by focusing on another child in the family (Minuchin, Rosman, and Baker, 1978). This may allow the symptomatic child to move in a more autonomous direction.

Families Who Relate Like Strangers: The Pain of Disconnection

At the other end of the continuum from enmeshed families are disengaged families. Families who are distant and disconnected from each other have too much space between them and the family therapist attempts to create proximity. When children are placed outside of the home and then brought back together for family therapy sessions, they sometimes relate like strangers. They may have been apart for long stretches of time and hardly know one another. The goal is to work on reconciliation of the family and to focus the interactions on the parent trying to understand the children better, their worries, sense of alienation and loneliness and the hurt they feel. Often the parent and child will need coaching because they really don't know how to talk or relate to each other, even when there is a strong longing to do so. In this clinical scenario the coaching and intuitive skill of the therapist are important. It is important not to push too strongly, too quickly toward reconciliation until the family members have had an opportunity to experiment; the children expressing their anger, the parents expressing their guilt in the presence of the therapist who can modulate the intensity. Strong affect can be readily communicated only in those family relationships, which have a deep root of trust.

In families that are chaotic and disorganized it is often important to work on the relationships first and build attachments before focusing the parents on implementing structure and discipline. The goal is to work on reconciliation of the family and to focus the interactions on the parent trying to understand the children better, their worries, their sense of alienation and loneliness and the hurt they feel inside.

The therapist can focus questions on relational issues such as: "Did you feel you found out more about your son's worries?" "Did you feel you got any closer to understanding what he is hurting about?" It is important to pursue the underlying pain and to support the parent(s) in staying with it so they can develop more of a connection with their child. Any parenting education around discipline or child management issues will have a better chance of success if the relationship is developed first.

In the families who are disengaged, it is sometimes helpful for the therapist to try to engage with each family member separately then gradually help them to engage with each other. In family therapy the therapist may have intense moments of contact with individual family members but they should be brief and less frequent than the intensity of the connections that the therapist tries to facilitate between family members.

In families of documented trauma there may be parts of the story that the child has never told the parent(s) and will not do so unless the parent(s) convinces the child that they really want to hear it. Usually, since these situations are exceedingly painful to the family, the therapist will bring up the hard topics that need to be addressed. If the therapist waits for the family to bring it up, it may never happen because it is simply too hard for them to initiate discussion of topics like abuse, violence, trauma, death, serious health problems, or drug or alcohol addiction.

It is crucial to help parents understand how children think, the kinds of worries and fears they often have and to get the parents curious about what is going on in their heads so the children are not struggling alone with all of this scary stuff. If, for example, a mother had a series of unhappy relationships with men and due to violence or drinking or some other problem she threw them out of the house, you can bet her son's worry is: "Will I be next?" With the traffic of males in and out of the house it is a natural worry but sometime parents need coaching to help children to bring these worries out in the open because they are inclined to bear them alone in order to protect the parent.

In situations where there is a significant disconnection it is important that the clinician appreciate that events have taken place in the life of the parental figure(s) which have precipitated the disconnection. The clinician is always inquiring of self, "I wonder how the parent has been doing as a woman, as a person in her own right?" Invariably the road has been difficult, and the parent has not been given the opportunity to open up to an interested other adult.

Children Caught in the Crossfire—Devastating Wounds to the Soul of the Child

Consider the following scenario:

The tension in the room is palpable. Two parents who hate each other and are locked into a bitter feud regarding the custody of the children and financial matters. They are in and out of court constantly accusing one or the other of some misdeed. The boundary between them and their children is way off and the children are embroiled and enmeshed in the emotional soup between the parents and this soup is toxic to the children.

The parents can't let go of the emotionality between them. The parents in their hurt and anger toward one another do not see what this is doing to their children. The battles go on, meanwhile, the children suffer anguish and torment beyond belief as they witness each parent trying to demolish the other.

As Silverstein (1995) pointed out when there is this much bitterness and animosity, the parties are not emotionally finished with each other, we have to help them finish it. A family was seen many years ago after the father ended up in the hospital with a broken skull. The parents had separated and reunited twelve times after stormy, violent battles. Finally, their sixteen-year-old son couldn't take it anymore, and in the middle of a fight between the father and mother, he hit his father over the head with a glass soda bottle. Sadly, his four-year-old sister had ulcers. Both children were casualties on the front-line of the parental war.

When Children Tyrannize the Family—The Wounds Are Externalized

Parents may allow the child to tyrannize the family if parents in their own families were victimized. At times in family therapy a mother is observed who is almost completely walled off from her children. It is very unusual to see a mother so disengaged from her children. All of the children are typically symptomatic and acting-out at home.

The therapist may at a properly timed moment need to say, "I wonder what happened to you that you are so disengaged, disconnected, so unattached. We have not been able to make a connection with you perhaps because we have not properly recognized the trauma you have been through and how hard your life has been." In such cases the children may feel relieved that the therapist has brought this into the open and often the acting-out behavior of the children will begin to subside.

Sometimes in families it is necessary to be quite direct and confront the unhealthy pattern in the family. If for example, a parent is unable to be authoritative it might be necessary for the therapist to say something like, "Mrs. Smith (fictional name) talk to your daughter about three things that worry you about her behavior. Talk to her about how you want her to behave when it comes to fighting with her brother or sister. Mrs. Smith, do you realize that you are debating with your daughter? She is five and you are thirty-two. Don't you think it would work better if you were the parent and provide direction to your little girl?"

It is also important for the therapist to directly clarify issues related to substance abuse and violence in the families. The therapist might say, "I need you to be straight with me about this drinking issue. How much of a problem is it really? Do you drive and drink? Your kids are worried about your drinking. Has anyone else expressed concern about your drinking?" With respect to violence, the therapist might say, "You seem like a nice and likeable guy. I can't fathom that you apparently were hitting your wife (or kids). You seem like a good guy—either you are fooling me or you've learned your lesson. Which is it?"

Consider the following scenario:

The family in the therapy room is chaotic. No one listens to anyone. The children are out of control. Mom is a single parent overwhelmed with her four small children. She means well but doesn't have the tools to make a connection with her nine-year-old son Kyle who has been acting out in increasingly dangerous ways. The therapist might encourage her to talk to Kyle, "Mrs. Wilson (fictional name), I want you to talk with your son right now. Help him to share some of the things that are difficult for him to think about or to feel. Ask him about some of the things he worries about—ask him to talk to you about his worries. See that Mrs. Wilson, he is spinning in his chair. What do you make of this? See if you can help him to talk about his worries. Don't you think he is the kind of boy that has been sad and lonely? He has a lot of worries. I think he has a lot of worries about you. Tell him you really want to know what is making him sad." So often in our experience the heart to heart connection is sorely longed for but family members simply don't know how. They can talk if we structure the communication. It is up to us to help them connect in a meaningful, heart-to-heart exchange.

When a Parent Can't Parent

Sometimes the therapist's desire to unite parents and their child is stronger than the parents.' This may be the case when a parent doesn't want to be a parent because she/he never had a childhood. Sometimes these parents are afraid of their own aggression around the child because the child is needy and pulling for something from them and they feel they have nothing to give. Often the children need nurturing when they become testy just before they act-out in a more serious way, but the parents may not understand that or be unable to give it.

Parent management training (Kazdin, 2005) is an empirically supported intervention with parents of children with behavior problems taking the form of oppositional, defiant, and aggressive behavior. With parents of acting-out children it is sometimes better to work with the parent(s) alone for a while. If the parents feel joined with, supported, and respected they will often be able to be more supportive, nurturing and caring with their children.

These families need to have someone listen to their stories. When we hear their stories, what we will learn is that many of these parents were traumatized in their early lives as well.

Empathy for Families and Respect for Family Healing Resources

Many of the families of children with significant emotional pain face harsh economic circumstances, deprivation, unemployment, and lack of educational opportunities. In many cases the parents were victims of abuse or exposure to violence growing up in their families, neighborhoods, and communities. Others were subjugated to various oppressive forces, such as racial, class or gender discrimination. Still others are ravaged with the devastating consequences of alcohol and/or drug addiction. If we adopt a judgmental or blaming posture, we will never be able to understand or help these families.

Mary Pipher's (2005) warning should be taken seriously by all therapists. Pipher stated, "When we alienate clients from their families we assume an enormous responsibility. If we take away belief in family, what do we replace it with? If people don't trust their families, who is it they can trust?" (2005, p. 30)

Minuchin also cautions family therapists to not pathologize families especially when they are going through transitional periods. He explained, "The period after the separation is always stressful for family members. They must negotiate new patterns of functioning while the blueprints that governed the old family still control their habitual responses. Family therapists who see families in the period of transition may misdiagnose the search for new patterns and the ensuing pain. We may label as deviant what is actually the creative attempt of a family organism to develop a new shape—the shedding and becoming that precede a butterfly" (Minuchin, 1984, p. 20).

Most parents love their children, and do the best they can for their families. We admire and respect their courage, their strength, and perseverance against what at times seem impossible obstacles. When you live in abject poverty, it is a slippery slope to climb out. Just when you think you are getting ahead, the car breaks down, one of the children gets sick and you incur major medical bills or perhaps you lose your job.

Hardy (2005) observed that low-income families suffer devaluation. They have been valued negatively by the dominant culture. The consequences of devaluation often lead to shame, secrecy and silencing. We witness the struggles of these families and marvel at their faith, and ability to carry on.

Family therapists would be well served to remember the wise counsel of Mary Pipher who observed, "Families for all their flaws are one of our remaining ancient and true shelters. Families, not therapists, will be there for our clients if they lose their jobs, go to the hospital, or need someone to show up at their bowling tournaments" (Pipher, 2005, p. 31).

We conclude this chapter by remembering the final sentence in Thornton Wilder's (1927) Pulitzer Prize winning novel, *The Bridge of San Luis Rey.* Wilder stated, "There is a land of the living and a land of the dead and the bridge is love, the only survival, the only meaning" (p. 148). It is love and connection with others that makes life meaningful and worthwhile. Our families can in the best of circumstances provide the "shelter for the soul" described in the next chapter that all human beings long for and in the worst of circumstances can be the source of unbelievable destructiveness and inflict the most devastating of all blows to the child's spirit.

REFERENCES

Crenshaw, D. A. (1990). *Bereavement: Counseling the grieving throughout the life cycle.* New York: Continuum [1995] reprinted by Crossroads Publishing, New York [2002] reprinted by Wipf & Stock Publishers, Eugene, OR.

Crenshaw, D. A. (2005). Clinical tools to facilitate treatment of childhood traumatic grief. *Omega: Journal of Death & Dying, 51,* 239–55.

Fraiberg, S., Adelson, E., & Shapiro, V. (1965). Ghosts in the nursery. *Journal of the American Academy of Child Psychiatry, 14,* 387–424.

Garbarino, J. (1999). *Lost boys: Why our sons turn violent and how we can save them.* New York: Anchor Books, A Division of Random House.

Hardy, K. V. (2005). *Working with low-income families.* Presentation at the Ackerman Institute for the Family. New York.

Imber-Black, E. & Papp, P. (2000). *Betrayals and reconciliations.* Presentation at the Psychotherapy Network Symposium. Washington, DC.

Kazdin, A. E. (2005). *Parent management training: Treatment for oppositional, aggressive, and antisocial behavior in children and adolescents.* New York: Oxford University Press.

McGoldrick, M. (1998). *Making remarried families work.* A presentation at the Family Therapy Networker Symposium. Washington, DC.

Minuchin, S. (1984). *Family kaleidoscope.* Cambridge, MA: Harvard University Press.

Minuchin, S., & Fishman, H. C. (1981). *Family therapy techniques.* Cambridge, MA: Harvard University Press.

Minuchin, S., & Nichols, M. P. (1993). *Family healing: Tales of hope and renewal from family therapy.* New York: The Free Press.

Minuchin, S., Rosman, B. L., & Baker, L. (1978). *Psychosomatic families: Anorexia Nervosa in context.* Cambridge, MA: Harvard University Press.

Papp, P. (1983). *The process of change.* New York: Guilford Press.

Pipher, M. (2005). *Letters to a young therapist.* New York: Basic Books.

Silverstein, O. (1987). *The art of systems therapy.* A presentation at the Ackerman Institute for the Family. New York.

Silverstein, O. (1995). *Inclusion/Exclusion.* A presentation at the Ackerman Institute for the Family. New York.

Trozzi, M., & Massimini, K. (1999). *Talking with children about loss.* New York: Perigee Books.

Wilder, T. (1927). *The bridge of San Luis Rey.* New York: Harper & Row. Reprinted (1986). New York: Perrenial Library.

Wylie, M. S. (2005). Maestro of the consulting room. *Psychotherapy Networker, 29,* 40–50.

4

Seeking a Shelter for the Soul: Healing the Wounds of Spiritually Empty Children

James Garbarino and David A. Crenshaw

OVERVIEW

The frantic, obsessive pursuit of a better material life was mentioned in Chapter 1 as a source of stress in today's world for both adults and our youth. Historian, Mark Lytle, in America's Uncivil Wars (2006) observed that concern about America's preoccupation with materialism was a source of cultural conflict in the 1960s with the youth counterculture rejecting the single-minded pursuit of material acquisitions by their parents. In contemporary America, however, youth as mentioned in Chapter 1, seem to be fully inducted into the values of materialism and many suffer from spiritual emptiness, alienation, and loneliness. In addition the emphasis on the buried potential of youth in this chapter is reflected in the strategies that are designed to honor the strengths of children in Chapter 5.

John O'Donohue (1999) refered to home as ideally a "shelter for the soul." Many children we have known in foster care express a compelling desire "to return home." In working with the families of these children it becomes clear that this theme could easily express the struggle of the entire family. Hardy (2000) discussed the concept of "psychological homelessness," a child, a family adrift in the world without a true sense of home, of roots. The child is seeking a secure place, a physical as well as spiritual home, from parents who in many cases never experienced this either. In effect the entire family is suffering from "psychological homelessness." And this issue touches on the core concept of social maps.

SOCIAL MAPS

Children live in and through their social maps. Each map is both the prod-
uct of past experience and the cause of future experience. Some children see
themselves as powerful, secure countries, surrounded by allies. Others see
themselves as poor little islands, surrounded by an empty ocean or hostile
enemies.

Such representations of the world reflect a child's intellectual ability—
the cognitive competence of knowing the world in an objective sense—
but they also indicate moral and emotional inclinations. Children develop social maps, and then they live by them. In early childhood, the
outlines of these social maps begin to emerge. What we commonly call
"attachment" is the first such map. It reflects the way an infant under-
stands the social environment.

Some infants have a strong, positive map of attachment and live a life of
responsiveness and security. For them it provides a foundation for exploration—physically and emotionally—because it provides a secure base for
human operations, a secure mini-homeland.

Without this starting point in attachment, the human being is psychologically homeless, and the social map begins to merge without appropriate boundaries, allies, and orientation to emotional north, south, east, and
west. Cultures differ in the precise components of these early social maps.
For example in some societies, fathers provide intimate care for infants and
emerge in their attachments early on, whereas in other societies fathers do
not appear in childhood social maps until later on. But the universal truth
is that someone must be "on the map."

The psychoanalyst Erik Erikson proposed that children must find their
way through a series of major challenge en route to a healthy adulthood.
These "crises" require that the child construct a social map that will show
the way. The first potential roadblock is "basic trust vs. mistrust." Does
the child come to know the world as a reliable place, where needs are
met (basic trust), or as a chaotic place where needs go unmet (basic
mistrust).

If children can navigate through this challenge, they continue down the
road of development. Other potential roadblocks lie ahead, such as failing
to become competent in dealing with bodily issues like toilet training as a
toddler, failing to develop a balanced approach to adult authority as a
school-aged child, and, as we shall see later, failing to develop a solid positive identity as an adolescent.

The social map continues to develop in ways that reflect the child's experiences and emerging capacities. What is more, the social map more and
more becomes the cause of experience. By adolescence, a youth is acting
constantly upon the basis of the information within the map. The youth

whose map contains allies, acts confidently and securely, and increasingly finds the positive place in life. The youth whose map renders him or her an insignificant speck stuck off in a corner, accrues more and more negative experiences.

We are concerned about the conclusions about the world contained in a youth's social map. Will it be "Adults are to be trusted because they know what they are doing," "People will generally treat you well and meet your needs," "I am a valued member of my society," and "The future looks bright to me? Or, will it be "Strangers are dangerous," "School is a dangerous place," "I feel all alone," and "All I see in my future is more disappointment and failure"?

Just what are the boundaries of a child's social map? All the great spiritual teachers from all the world's faith traditions teach us that the boundaries are not limited to the material and observable world. They extend outward to the universe and inward to the heart. But how are we to study and understand these non-material dimensions.

SPIRITUAL NEEDS OF CHILDREN AND THE LONGING FOR "HOME"

Human beings are spiritual beings and thus have spiritual needs. No simply material conception of human identify will suffice. This is a vitally important recognition for understanding the quality of the world outside our front door. And, this is very different from speaking about religion. There are those who are religious but not spiritual—and vice versa. To recognize our spiritual needs is to recognize that we have a fundamental need to know we live in a meaningful universe, that there is something more to our lives than the material experience of those lives. This becomes apparent when we consider the social maps of children and youth regarding home, being at home and feeling at home.

The secure, protective, nurturing nest that we think of as home has often not been available for multiple generations within the families of severely troubled children and the lack of roots and secure attachments pervades the family's psychological struggle to find what has always been missing from their individual and collective lives (Crenshaw and Garbarino, 2007). Those of us who were provided a secure base (Bowlby, 1969), a "psychological home," in early life are privileged. Since the need to feel secure, safe, and protected is so basic we probably take it for granted, but so many have not experienced this. Thus, they are in a never-ending quest to find the home of their longing or in some cases to return to the home they once had but lost along the way. They are longing for and seeking a "shelter for the soul."

In his poem, "The Death of the Hired Hand," Robert Frost offered a succinct introduction to this question when he wrote,

> Home is the place where
> when you have to go there
> they have to take you in.

H. L. Mencken offered a more formal introduction when he wrote, "A home is not a mere transient shelter. Its essence lies in its permanence, in its capacity for accretion and solidification, in its quality of representing, in all its details, the personalities of the people who live in it."

The focal point of both Frost's and Mencken's observations is that "home" implies permanence and stability. You have a home when you have a place to go, no matter what. You have a home when you are connected permanently with a place that endures and represents your family. As a young homeless child wrote, "A home is where you can grow flowers if you want."

The Secure Family Base

Byng-Hall (2002) proposed the concept of a secure family base that he defined as "a family that provides a network of sufficiently reliable attachment relationships so that members of the family, of whatever age, are able to feel secure" (p. 376). Byng-Hall delineated factors that undermine the security of the family base, including marital conflicts, blurring of generational boundaries including destructive parentification and cross-generational coalitions.

Mothers of children who are classified as manifesting insecure/disorganized attachment in the Strange Situation (SS) have been found to be more prone to abdication of parenting (George & Solomon, 1999). These mothers perceive themselves as being helpless to protect their child from threats or danger, and often view themselves as being out of control.

Children who are terrified by their parent's maltreatment will not be able to turn to the parent for comfort, soothing or protection since the parent is also the source of the fear. These insecure/disorganized-attached children have been found to be an especially vulnerable group of children (Solomon & George, 1999). If children miss out on a secure base, a "psychological home," in early development it is expected that they will have major struggles around attachment and will be fearful of any further separation or loss or even the threat of it.

For young children, the concept of home is closely allied with the concept of family. In fact, for very young children, it is hard to separate the two: "my home is where my family lives." Like turtles, young children carry their homes around with them, as they are carried along by their families. This is important to know. It highlights the importance of social disruption in the lives of parents as a threat to children. Anything that affects the availability of parents and their ability to create and sustain a home for a young child is bad news.

Research on children in war zones around the world tells us that young children can cope well with the stress of social upheaval if they retain strong positive attachments to their families, and if parents can continue to project a sense of stability, permanence, and competence to their children.

One implication is that when parents of young children have trouble functioning (which may be linked to their sense of being homeless), we can expect negative effects on those children. It is difficult for a family to function well without a home (both in the narrow sense of having a permanent residence and in the larger sense of being part of an intact community).

This is one way to interpret Kai Erikson's study of families who lost their homes and their community as the result of a devastating flood. In his 1976 book, *Everything in Its Path*, Erikson highlighted the subsequent difficulties encountered by these families who sought simultaneously to build new homes and a new community. His study directs our attention to the intense social toxicity that arises when whole communities become uprooted. For very young children the principal danger is that a demolished community will demoralize their parents.

For older children and for adolescents there is another danger, that the lack of community itself will prove harmful. But the story is not simple. These traumatic events can later become the basis for spiritual and psychological growth and development in later life if there is a process of therapeutic recovery.

Home Is Extended to Community

Once children leave the period of infancy and early childhood (at approximately age eight), their well-being comes to depend more and more upon social realities beyond the immediate family. Their experiences extend in wider circles beyond the family into the neighborhood and the community. At the same time, home becomes more than family. It includes school, neighborhood, and friends.

Children appreciate being home in new and different ways as they develop. For a child to have a home is for that child to have a family that lives somewhere, that belongs someplace. A family with a home has a place to call its own (putting aside matters like legal ownership, which are virtually meaningless to a child). Such a family may recognize the possibility of moving in the future to another place, but carries with it the expectation that this new place will become a new home.

Why does the young child equate home and family? It follows from the
limited ability of young children to engage in abstract thinking. Young children think in concrete terms, and this concrete thinking makes it likely that
"home" and "family" will be the same. What about older children? For
them, home and family are separable. A friend announced her intention of
selling her home and moving to a new apartment once her daughter grad-
uated from high school and moved on to college. "But I'll never have a
home again," her daughter lamented.

One adult recalls his own loss of "home" 40 years earlier, with the
kind of vividness that only emotionally laden memories can sustain.
When he was 18 his parents moved from the house in which he had lived
since he was seven years old to a new community 20 miles away. The
move took place while he was away at college, so when Thanksgiving
break came he traveled to the new house but knew that he could never
go home again as a child. He knew that only by getting married and having children of his own could he really have a home again. His children
felt the same way when they moved from one city to another in 1985.
They had a roof over their heads yet they felt homeless during the transitional period. The father recalls with pain suggesting to his then twelve-
year-old daughter one day that we "go home" (to the new apartment)
and her replying, "I have no home." It took time and experience to make
the new house a home.

"New home" is a shaky concept, a contradiction in terms. This is what
this girl was telling us. For a child to accept a new home is an act of faith.
The child is asked to believe that a new place will become a home. A new
home is an expectation of stability, a promise not a fact. It is a commitment
to put down roots to build relationships, memories, traditions, associations, and images. This is what it means to tell a child that he or she is home
in a new house and neighborhood. For a child, home is a crucial feature of
the social map, and when it is missing, the child may be set adrift and put
in jeopardy. Children in foster care face these issues with a special
poignancy.

Andre, a seven-year-old child in residential treatment, has had four prior
psychiatric hospitalizations for suicide attempts, aggressive and violent behavior. He had been in numerous foster homes that were unable to contain
him. He was in one foster home that appeared to be working and he became attached to his foster mother, but she became ill and he had to be removed to another home. His biological parents are crack-addicted and have
surrendered their parental rights. When children this young are so seriously
symptomatic they have usually been exposed to repeated profound losses
and often exposed to violence and trauma. They have never or rarely experienced a true sense of "home."

Longing for Home: A Powerful Theme in Literature

Thomas Wolfe's (1940) compelling novel, *You Can't Go Home Again*, is a story of the longing for an idealized home that either never was or can no longer be. It is a story of George Webber, a writer, who writes a successful novel about his hometown and then returns. He is astounded and shaken by the outrage of the hometown folks who felt exposed by what he had written in his books and their rage drives him from his home. *Psychologically homeless* children often long for a romanticized view of the past that never was and can never be in the future. In Wolfe's classic, it can be speculated that George Webber's desire to return to his hometown was significantly influenced by his father's abandonment of the family for another woman, and by his mother's death from a "broken heart." The futility of his return to his hometown may have been highly determined by his seeking the "home of his longing," his quest for a "shelter for his soul," a home that never was a reality for him.

In Steinbeck's (1938) powerful novel, *Of Mice and Men*, Lenny, an intellectually impaired giant of a man and his companion and guardian George, drifters working as ranch hands, dream that some day they will acquire a piece of land and a home of their own. They cling to each other to counter the alienation and loneliness they both feel while holding on to their dream. This is a novel of the tragic crushing of one's hopes and cherished dreams. The dream of working hard and being able to change one's life is a core value held by many Americans. In fact, all of the characters in Steinbeck's novel cling to the dream of changing their lives. The dream is different for each person, but the hope is for a better way of living, and in George and Lenny's case, a home that they can call their own. None of the characters succeed. In the character of Crooks, Steinbeck conveys the anger, bitterness, and powerlessness of the African American who struggles to be treated as a human being, let alone have a place of his own. The title which refers to Robert Burns, a Scottish poet's verse, "The best laid schemes of mice and men often go awry," lays the foundation for the sad conclusion of the book and the overriding theme that to dream leads to despair.

When George mercifully puts a gun in the back of Lenny's head and pulls the trigger to spare Lenny a lynching by an angry posse in hot pursuit after Lenny accidentally killed the ranch foreman's wife, Lenny asks George in the moment prior to death, to once again describe the home that someday will be theirs. The dream was kept alive until the very end, but when George pulled the trigger, he lost both his companion and their jointly shared dream. He was then forced to face the sad truth along with his migrant farm co-workers, as well as so many who live along the margins of society, that one has to surrender one's dreams in order to survive. It is not possible to continue to dream of a home of one's own, because the repeated destruction of that dream is too painful to bear.

Steinbeck's (1939) epic story, *The Grapes of Wrath*, depicted the lives of ordinary people facing the horrors of the Great Depression. The Joad family lose their tenant farm and joins thousands of others, traveling the narrow highways out to California to seek the dream of a better life, a piece of land to call their own. Like George and Lenny, the migrant farmhands in *Of Mice and Men*, the dreams of the Joads for a better life are not fulfilled as they face further setbacks and losses along their journey. The hardships and economic oppression suffered by migrant laborers during the Great Depression is vividly detailed in the story. The novel describes the conditions in Dust Bowl, Oklahoma that ruined the crops and led to massive foreclosures by banks on farmland.

Another powerful theme in this classic Steinbeck novel is that in spite of the hardships and the struggle for survival the Joad family, inspired by Ma Joad, the cohesive force of the family, manages to maintain their pride and sense of dignity. Steinbeck through the novel's main characters emphasizes the importance of maintaining self-respect in order to survive emotionally and spiritually. In this novel, Steinbeck illustrates what has been a powerful theme in therapy with many contemporary inner city youth, the inextricable link between attacks on dignity and rage. The lifestyle of the migrant workers makes the quest for a home both a burning desire and an utterly unattainable dream. Life on the road entailed incomparable and repeated losses that decimated the family units, and without a home to define its boundaries, facing persecution and looked upon in a dehumanized manner, their hopes and dreams were crushed and turned into despair. Their quest for a home and a better life was shattered, reduced to wrath and ground to dust.

The Longing for Home: A Powerful Theme in Therapy

In therapy we try to reconnect people to their past, to their core self, to their family and other important people in their lives and to the extent we are successful that is the closest we may come to helping them find their way home. Those who are disconnected are at sea and a long way from home. Meaningful closeness with others is what makes life's burdens bearable and without that buffering influence life for many is intolerably painful.

Young *psychologically homeless* children play out over and over in their fantasy play the theme of seeking home. More than fifty years ago Winnicott (1948) described the problem of trying to settle children in homes outside of London during the bombings of World War II. He described how the children who had experienced what he called a "good primary home" experience were able to adapt and adjust in their temporary homes. These children had come from basically stable families and had established a sense of basic trust that their needs would be met. Children, however, who had missed out on an adequate primary home experience, had a difficult time adjusting and settling into the temporary homes. Winnicott suggested that the children who had missed out on secure early attachments were not able to trust that their basic needs would be met, held a fantasy of what their idealized and longed for home would be, and compared to that idealized image no actual home could measure up.

This resembles the plight of children in out-of-home placements regardless of the reason. Winnicott (1948) studied children who had been removed to escape the bombings. Many children are removed from their homes to foster care to escape the violence either within their families, or neighborhoods, and communities. Children in residential treatment centers often experience home visits with intense ambivalence. On the one hand, they long for reunion; on the other hand, they fear that nothing will have changed and their dream of a safe place, a material as well as psychological or spiritual home, will once again be crushed.

A typical play scenario consists of a warrior returning from battle and trying to make his way home. Along the way he gets lost and finds himself in foreign or enemy territory that is far from home. Some of the most intensely fought wars in their play scenarios are over the attempts to capture their native land and return the people to their rightful homes. This is one of the most powerful themes played out by *psychologically homeless* children, the quest to return "home," in many cases the longed for home, the safe place, they never had.

A six-year-old girl plays out the following scenario. A major car crash occurs outside the school and outside the home. The teacher tries to block the windows with the blackboard so the children can't see the horrible crash. At home the mother puts a table in the window to block the scene of the crash. But these attempts to protect the children fail. The kids at school wanting to see what had happened went outside while the teacher was reading a story, but they weren't listening because they were too worried about the crash. The dinosaurs knocked down the house but only the baby was inside with the mother. Even though the house was knocked down no one was hurt. The children at school, however, did not survive because the dinosaurs devoured them. The rescue vehicles on the way back to the garage after doing everything they could collide with each other and the taxi and the police car crashed into each other.

The child then abruptly shifted to healing play whereby she became a kind and caring doctor who gave the patient (therapist) painful shots but they healed his illness. In the above play scenario the child is revealing that her world (home and school) is under attack. This child had been exposed to considerable domestic violence that led to the break-up of the family and an order of protection against her father. She is of school age so she plays out her fear that she will not survive the assault of the domestic violence (dinosaurs eating the schoolchildren and turning over the home). Her little sister, however, home alone with her mother and perhaps too young to fully comprehend the situation seems to be faring better. Of course, the dinosaurs turning over the home with mother and baby in it could represent the child's hostility toward her younger sister, too young to go to school and getting all of that additional attention from mother. This was quickly undone, however, in that miraculously neither mother nor baby was hurt when the house turned over.

The child, obviously anxious, abruptly shifted play to a healing theme that expresses considerable hope, although painful work is required (shots) for the patient to get well. When one's home is under attack, it becomes the dominant preoccupation of the child. The children couldn't listen to the teacher reading the story and had to venture out to see what was happening as a result of the crash in spite of the teacher's efforts to protect them.

The play scenario also captures the futility of parents protecting the child (mother putting the table to block the window; the teacher using the blackboard to do the same at school) when the crash is just outside their door. We have known families where the children were exposed to repeated incidents of domestic violence and yet the parents were in denial as to whether the children even knew about the fights let alone were affected by them.

Whether, the therapy is with children, adolescents, or adults, the quest for a spiritual refuge, a warm, protective nest, a nurturing, secure place, a "shelter for the soul" is often a powerful theme, particularly for those children, youth, and adults who missed out on such a safe and nourishing haven when they needed it most, in the early part of their lives when crucial attachment experiences facilitate the development not only of our neurobiology and critical centers of the brain, but our very being, our connectedness with others and the world, it shapes our spirit, our core sense of self.

Home under Attack

An almost universal wish on that horrific day, September 11, 2001, even among some of the heroic fire and police and rescue personnel, who like many throughout the nation bravely carried on the work that had to be done, was the wish to somehow get home and be with their family. But what if you do not have a home, at least a safe home? The place that is supposed to be refuge, a safe haven, may be under attack. The brutal forces of poverty, discrimination, violence either within the home or the neighborhood or both, are mounting a frontal assault on what most of us take for granted, that home is a place of safety and refuge. In the inner city wars some families dive to the living room floor to dodge bullets in the night that stray from a gunfight in the streets. What has happened to the refuge that all children need when they come into this world and continue to need during their vulnerable developmental years? For some children and families the refuge, the safe haven was never there.

SEEKING A SPIRITUAL HOME—A SHELTER FOR THE SOUL

Children are craving for more than just a material world (Garbarino, 1999). "Kids feel a sense of purposefulness when they are rooted in a world that makes sense. It makes sense to follow the rules if you feel the authority that makes the rules has your interests at heart. It makes sense to respect your elders if you see them as powerful, well-intentioned, in charge of the world in which you live, and benevolent toward you. It makes sense to work hard if you see hard work rewarded. It makes sense to love—if you know what it feels like to be loved" (Garbarino, 1999, pp. 153–54).

Confusion and Lack of Training Regarding Spirituality

In the mental health field there is much confusion as to what is meant by spirituality and the mental health disciplines provide little formal training in spirituality. Bregman (2006) noted both the popularity of the term spirituality and its multiple uses that keep its exact meaning blurred. Bergman argued that the term is the latest in a long search for a personal and positive dimension of religion within the context of a secularized society. Russell and Yarhouse (2006) pointed out that since the vast majority of Americans have an allegiance to a particular faith tradition, it is important that psychologists have experience and training in working with clients who hold a wide range of religious/spiritual perspectives. Yet, when Russell and Yarhouse surveyed 139 American Psychological Association (APA) accredited internship sites they found that few provide formal training in religion/spirituality.

The Buffering Role of Spirituality

This issue becomes even more poignant when considering the central role that religion and spirituality play in the lives of low-income families and among minority families (Christian & Barbarin, 2001). Findings reported by Christian and Barbarin (2001) support the importance of religion as a sociocultural resource in African American families, one that potentially contributes to resilience of children at risk for behavioral or emotional maladjustment as a function of growing up in poor families and communities. Furthermore, increasing evidence suggests that religion and spiritual beliefs and practices promote mental health and positive correlations have been found between religious commitment and both physical and mental health (Gartner, 1996; Russell & Yarhouse, 2006) as indicated by lower rates of mortality, suicide, drug and alcohol abuse, delinquency and criminal behavior, divorce, and depression, as well as higher rates of well-being and marital satisfaction.

The Longing for a Spiritual Home

Every person needs a spiritual home. Some find peace, solace and uplifting of their spirit through their religious faith. The church, synagogue or mosque becomes their spiritual home. Others may find it in their love of nature, music, art, poetry, or writing. Where ever it is to be found and whatever form it takes, the nourishing of one's soul and the elevation of one's spirit is vital to surviving the hardships of life.

Anne Frank while in hiding with her family facing uncertainty and the likely prospect of death, somehow still managed to maintain a hopeful and positive philosophy of life. Since the publication of *The Diary of a Young Girl* in 1947, her story has been read by and provided inspiration to millions. She died three months short of her sixteenth birthday. This entry to her diary was on February 23, 1944 about five months before she and her family were captured:

> The best remedy for those who are afraid, lonely or unhappy is go outside, somewhere where they can be quiet, alone with the sky, nature and God. For then and only then can you feel that everything is as it should be and that God wants people to be happy amid nature's beauty and simplicity. As long as this exists, and that should be forever, I know that there will always be solace for every sorrow, whatever the circumstances. I firmly believe that nature can bring comfort to all who suffer. (Frank and Pressler, 1991, p. 196)

Then on the 15th of July, 1944 less than three weeks before the morning when an SS sergeant and members of the Dutch Security police arrived and arrested Anne and her family, she wrote, "It's difficult in times like these: ideals, dreams and cherished hopes rise within us, only to be crushed by grim reality. It's a wonder I haven't abandoned all my ideals; they seem so absurd and impractical. Yet I cling to them because I still believe, in spite of everything, that people are truly good at heart" (Frank and Pressler, 1991, p. 332).

Anne and her sister Margot died a few days apart from an outbreak of an epidemic that broke out in the concentration camp in Germany during the following winter that killed thousands of prisoners due to the horrendous hygienic conditions in the camps. Of the eight people hiding in the house, only her father Otto Frank survived the concentration camps. Anne Frank's courage, positive philosophy of life, her abiding belief in the goodness of her fellow human beings is one of the great testaments of the remarkable spirit and resilience of children. Even as she hid with her family in the back of an Amsterdam warehouse for two years she had found the most secure of all shelters, "a shelter for the soul."

Beverly James (1989) emphasized the crucial role of spirituality in providing an anchor to children scarred by abuse and neglect. James stated, "Children who have experienced profound and frightening changes in their lives, such as loss of a home or a parent, need to know they are more than their families, their possessions or their bodies. They need to feel that there is an inner core to their being that cannot be lost or taken away, and they have an inner wisdom upon which they can rely" (p. 211).

When there is an absence of a spiritual home, it is a major loss and leaves the child and/or family without an anchor to face the inevitable storms of life. If one has a spiritual home, it is to be treasured, nurtured, visited often, and valued for the refuge it truly is in the midst of life's adversities. In working with severely wounded children, there is perhaps no greater contribution we can make, than to help them find within a spiritual home, a place of inner sanctuary, an internal haven bound not by a white picket fence but by their own unique essence and specialness, a place of healing and inner peace, a "shelter for the soul" that can never, ever be taken away.

REFERENCES

Bowlby, J. (1969). *Attachment and loss, Vol. I. Attachment.* London: Hogarth Press.

Bregman, L. (2006). Spirituality: A glowing and useful term in search of a meaning. *Omega: Journal of Death and Dying, 53,* 5–26.

Byng-Hall, J. (2002). Relieving parentified children's burdens in families with insecure attachment patterns. *Family Process, 41,* 375–88.

Christian, M. D., & Barbarin, O. A. (2001). Cultural resources and psychological adjustment of African American children: Effects of spirituality and racial attribution. *Journal of Black Psychology, 27,* 43–63.

Crenshaw, D. A., & Garbarino, J. (2007). The hidden dimensions: Profound sorrow and buried human potential in violent youth. *Journal of Humanistic Psychology, 47,* 160–74.

Erickson, K. (1976). *Everything in its path-Destruction of community in the Buffalo Creek Flood.* New York: Simon & Schuster.

Frank, O. H. & Pressler, M. (Eds.) (1991). *Anne Frank: The diary of a young girl.* New York: Doubleday.

Garbarino, J. (1999). *Lost boys: Why our sons turn violent and how we can save them.* New York: Anchor Books, A Division of Random House.

Gartner, J. (1996). Religious commitment, mental health, and prosocial behavior: A review of the empirical literature. In E. P. Shafranske (Ed.), *Religion and the clinical practice of psychology* (pp. 187–214). Washington, DC: American Psychological Association.

George, C., & Solomon, J. (1999). Attachment and caregiving: The caregiving behavioral system. In J. Cassidy & P. R. Shaver (Eds.), *Handbook of attachment: Theory, research, and clinical applications* (pp. 649–70). New York: Guilford Press.

Hardy, K. V. (2000). *Psychological homelessness.* Presentation at the Family Therapy Networker Symposium. Washington, D. C.

James, B. (1989). *Treating traumatized children: New insights and creative interventions.* Lexington, MA: Lexington Books.

Lytle, M. H. (2006). *America's uncivil wars.* New York: Oxford University Press.

O'Donohue, J. (1999). *Eternal echoes: Exploring our yearning to belong.* New York: HarperCollins Publishers.

O'Donohue, J. (1999). *Eternal Echoes: Celtic Reflections on Our Yearning to Belong.* New York: Perennial/HarperCollins.

Russell, S. R., & Yarhouse, M. A. (2006). Training in religion/spirituality within APA-Accredited Psychology Predoctoral Internships. *Professional Psychology: Research and Practice, 37,* 430–36.

Solomon, J., & George, C. (1999). Attachment disorganization. New York: Guilford Press.

Steinbeck, J. (1938). *Of mice and men.* New York: Viking Press.

Steinbeck, J. (1939). *Grapes of wrath.* New York: Viking Press.

Winnicott, D. (1948). Children's hostels in war and peace. *British Journal of Medical Psychology, 21,* 175–80.

Wolfe, T. (1940). *You can't go home again.* New York: Harper & Row.

5

"Diamonds in the Rough": A Strengths-Based Approach to Healing Children and Families

Susan Cristantiello, David A. Crenshaw, and Konstantinos Tsoubris

OVERVIEW

Mental health professionals are traditionally trained to "pounce on pathology" and "document damage." This results in viewing children and families through a narrow and restricted lens that obscures their vision of the strengths, positive qualities, and resources within children and families. Yet, in therapy potent leverage for change can be enlisted by building on the pre-existing strengths of clients, and identifying new ones that are not recognized by the child or the family.[1]

Important strengths reside both in the person and in their relational resources, their ability to make close and sustaining relationships with others. In contrast, to the emphasis on punitive approaches so prevalent in our culture, Currie (2004) in his interviews with today's youth discovered that a crucial turning point in the lives of these young people was learning or relearning how to care about themselves—to view themselves as people who mattered. In addition they needed to find opportunities in their interpersonal world to put their altered self-definition into practice. Clearly, these turning points are facilitated when "charismatic adults" are available to the adolescents (Brooks and Goldstein, 2004).

Drawing on a term coined by the late Dr. Julius Segal, Brooks and Goldstein explain and that a charismatic adult is an adult from whom a child can gather strength. In studies of resilience, the presence of at least one charismatic adult is one of the key factors enabling youth to overcome adversity in their lives (Brooks and Goldstein, 2004).

STRENGTHS IN OUR YOUTH

While our culture emphasizes punishment and correction, the research consistently shows that it is meaningful connections between youth and the key adults in their lives that enable young people to turn their lives around in a positive way (Currie, 2004). Deeply troubled youth are easily and quickly demoralized thereby making essential a strengths-based approach to parenting, education, and therapy, as described by Brooks and Goldstein (2004). Brooks (1993, 2003) urged parents, teachers, and therapists to look for "islands of competence" in children. Brooks is an eloquent spokesman for the strengths-based approach to healing our youth and has injected a refreshing and energizing perspective in our field to counter the dank, dark, and often dispiriting over-emphasis on pathology that leaves both helpers and the intended recipients of help feeling stuck and hopeless.

Walter Bonime emphasized repeatedly that we need to pay just as close attention to "what is right with a person" as we do to "what is wrong with the person." He stated forcefully in psychoanalytic supervision (Crenshaw), "It is psychoanalysis, not pathoanalysis." Furthermore, Bonime insisted that human beings use only a small proportion of the capacities available to them. He stated, "There is an enormous potential in human beings for fuller development, continuing and increasing mastery and creativity than is provided for in our culture" (Bonime, 1989, p. 38). Bonime viewed anxiety generated by competitiveness and cynicism in Western culture as major barriers to fuller realization of human potential.

We gain far more leverage for change when we punctuate strengths in our youth and their families. Kenneth Hardy in a personal communication (September, 2004) expressed this beautifully by stating, "When we recognize and honor what children have to give, to offer, to contribute—we elevate their spirit; when children feel they have nothing to give, to offer, to contribute—it punctures their spirit."

Merriam (2006) noted that the healing process is augmented when strengths are combined in a collaborative effort, "The compassionate counselor, physician, friend, or helper is a guide who leads the woman giving birth, the wounded victim of disaster, the injured or the dying person to connection with his or her own deepest strengths. In order to do this, the healer must also be firmly connected with his own strengths. Through the interconnection of the core strengths of both healer and wounded comes the ability to create a vision of new life" (p. 122).

A recent study of a strengths-based approach with adolescents showed good results in preventing substance abuse (Tebes, Feinn, Vanderploeg, Chinman, Shepard, Brabham, et al. 2007). Adolescents receiving the positive youth development after-school program in an urban setting were significantly more likely to view drugs as harmful at program exit, and exhibited significantly lower increases in alcohol, marijuana, other drug use, and any drug use 1 year after beginning the program.

Competence and Strengths in Families

The competence-based approach to family therapy (Waters and Lawrence, 1993) emphasized not only the strengths of the family, but also honors the family's vision, courage, and facilitates hope. Waters and Lawrence explained, "A competence approach offers a model for integrating pathology and health. It assumes that symptoms are adaptive attempts gone awry and that the motives and passions that yield problems have a healthy side, a side of powerful striving for mastery. That striving is what needs to be understood, redirected, and harnessed for positive change. This requires of both client and therapist an understanding of the healthy roots of the problematic elements and how they got distorted into unhealthy patterns" (1993, p. 9). They further explain, "People coming for therapy are often stuck in a vision of themselves that is narrow and joyless. We see the therapist's job as expanding that vision and then helping clients to develop a map for getting there" (p. 39).

We can't afford to underestimate the strengths of families. Minuchin noted, "I am not blind to the destructiveness of abusive power, and I know there are times when the weak must be protected and the ruthless controlled—by force, if necessary. But again and again, as I see families, I am amazed by the variety of resources people have and the ways they can change—that is, use their resources differently. This means accepting the possibilities and limitations in oneself and others. It means tolerating uncertainties and differences. It also means hope—for new ways of being together" (Minuchin and Nichols, 1993, p. 287).

A similar point was made by Waters and Lawrence (1993). They stated, "No one sets out to go on a bad journey, but many journeys end up badly. Fundamental to a competence approach is respect for people's healthy striving. There are many more healthy motives in people than we are taught to recognize. The urgency to love and be loved and to master what is put before us is universal, however distorted the presentations. It is the pursuit of those needs that keeps us going" (p. 8).

Froma Walsh (2007) delineated the core principles and value of a family and community resilience-oriented approach to recovery from traumatic loss when catastrophic events occur. Walsh contrasted individually based, symptom-focused approaches to trauma recovery, from the multi-systemic practice approach that contextualizes the distress in the traumatic experience and taps strengths and resources in relational networks to foster healing and posttraumatic growth. In keeping with the above theoretical and research findings, the authors adhere to a strengths-based approach that honors the resources and resilience of both youth and their families. The clinical vignettes to follow later in this chapter, the first five of which were drawn from the Coordinated Children's Service Initiative (CCSI) which is a program operated by the Astor Home for Children's (hereafter referred to as Astor) Community-Based Programs in Dutchess County, NY, illustrate how this takes shape in everyday clinical practice.

CCSI PHILOSOPHY, RATIONALE AND PLACE IN THE SPECTRUM OF COMMUNITY SERVICES

CCSI is a collaborative process with families and community agencies aimed at preventing out-of-home placement of high-risk children with emotional and behavioral problems. Children are identified as candidates from one of several service systems: mental health, juvenile justice, child welfare, and education. CCSI's role is to provide the structure to effectively coordinate community services and enhance family function. Our core values direct that our intervention be family driven, with families as partners and colleagues, and community based. In addition, CCSI believes in culturally competent, strengths-based and individualized care.

In Dutchess County we have a rich home-based service environment: Home Based Crisis Intervention, Preventive Services, Supportive and Intensive Case Management, a Waiver Program and CCSI. Of these programs, CCSI has the unique function of coordinating the working plan of the community agencies involved in a child's life. Often a number of service providers are working on separate needs and concerns. Parents can feel overwhelmed by the demands placed upon them by the array of providers, and by trying to coordinate the complex care of their child. Adding to this, agencies are often unaware of each other's part in the care of the child. This has the potential for the creation of disparate or conflicting service plans and it places the parent in the confusing position of having to satisfy multiple directives (and juggle multiple appointments) while trying to care for their child. At times an agency's use may be mandated and may not be seen as helpful or benign by families (for example, probation, child protective services, or school disciplinarians).

The crucial importance of coordinating in a thoughtful way the varied service providers was driven home in a dramatic way when one of the authors (Crenshaw) attended a presentation by Salvador Minuchin (1986, Philadelphia Child Guidance Clinic) when he discussed a family in which 18 different agencies were represented in working with a multi-problem family that included incest. Minuchin observed that there were so well-meaning helpers involved with the family that due to lack of coordination they were constantly getting in each other's way. What was even more remarkable, Minuchin observed that due to the beehive of helping activity around this family, the family itself was relieved of the necessity of change thus negating the value of their collective efforts.

Families may be uninformed of all of their rights, and the existence of agencies that act on a voluntary basis to support the child in times of crisis or hardship. CCSI's Network meeting introduces the family to these new providers (e.g., court advocates, educational advocates, benefits advisors) who may offset the tensions created by the disciplinary or investigative agents. Bringing all these people together in a low-stress environment provides an opportunity for everyone to meet each other and form a unified plan with the child and family.

As a precursor to this process CCSI must first obtain a knowledge base regarding the family's service history and present situation. To this end we perform an assessment of the family's needs and strengths and discover what steps they have already taken to ameliorate their circumstances. We do this in an initial home visit. The CCSI Coordinator (Cristantiello) is a clinician who uses her training to assess the level of coordinated care that is needed and who makes a personal connection with the child in order to discover often hidden strengths and talents. Observing the child's interactions with others in the home and being invited into their own space adds richness to this assessment not possible in a clinic setting. The CCSI Coordinator is accompanied by a CCSI Family Advocate, an individual who brings unique sensitivities to the interview based on their own experience of having once been a "person-in-the-system." Parents understand that they are entering into a new type of connection, more parallel than hierarchal. We ask the children to help, to tell us whatever they can to direct us in our search for service assistance.

The child is intrigued by the idea that what they want is important, and that we'll be working with them, not telling them what to do. After doing research to match their requests with appropriate and at times exciting possibilities, we ask the family's approval to invite these new providers to the Network Meeting. This serves not only to empower the family to take the lead in sculpting the intervention, but communicates that we are serious about following their directives. Sometimes the family will ask that an agency they are having difficulty with not be invited. We advise that the Network meetings may be a good place to have the "difficult" agent present since our goal is to help the family give voice to their concerns in a supportive and objective atmosphere, where they feel safeguarded and respected.

Once the meeting has taken place, CCSI begins the process of coordinating the plan and shepherding the connections outlined therein. We may revise or add to the plan when the family requests it, and we may support the plan with wraparound funds when needed. Often we may accompany the child or parent to an initial meeting with a new provider to promote an effective new connection or simply lend support. We continue to encourage the family to use a wide network of services and opportunities, so they will be able to access them confidently on their own for as long as is efficacious.

CLINICAL ILLUSTRATIONS
OF THE STRENGTHS-BASED APPROACH

Clinical Vignette # 1: "The Lump under the Burlap"

A teen-aged boy whose mother and father had each tried to manage him as best they could, with deteriorating success was referred (for an intake planning meeting in the community services program) to CCSI. The parents were separated, not amicably, and each had taken turns trying to deal with their son in the aftermath of his psychiatric hospitalization and numerous behavioral problems and incidents that had engendered much anguish for all. Assessments were performed and a Network Meeting was to be held to offer services to the family and to develop a workable plan. The impasse was that the teenager was in the middle of discouraged, disheartened parents who were skeptical of still more plans. The teen himself felt estranged from and rejected by his warring parents.

The challenge was how to get this family talking and motivated for another try. The assessments focus on strengths as well as problems, and in the assessment the therapist noted that one of the strengths the child identified was mechanics. He liked to take things apart and to see how they worked (as point of identification, his father was mechanical), and had asked the Coordinator (Cristantiello) where he might get a car engine to work on. I helped him look in the phone book, inconclusively, but noted the strength and the wish.

Just prior to the network meeting I received a call from each of the parents expressing their anxiety about being in the same room with one another and asking that their son be seated in between them. Not wishing to place the child literally between his parents and looking for a way to pull the family together for this single meeting I remembered the motor request. After a quick foray into a neighboring junk yard I was handed a small engine by curious, helpful attendants.

At the meeting a large burlap-covered lump was placed on the end of the table. The family entered the room with reluctance but they were all drawn to the mysterious shape. The child was invited to have a look, and reacted with obvious pleasure as he revealed the engine that he was assured was his. Most importantly, his self-identified strength was publicly supported, acknowledged by both his parents and the professionals gathered. The idea

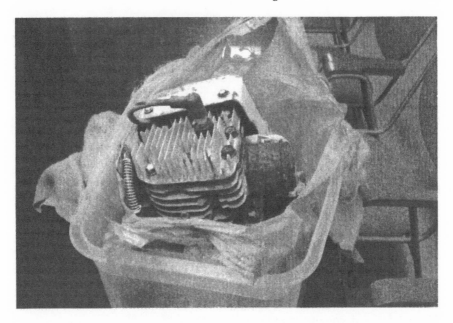

that he was truly heard by this system allowed him to participate fully in crafting a new plan with his parents and the professionals gathered, and allowed his parents and others to see him from an altered, more adaptive, perspective.

Clinical Vignette # 2: "Looking for a Needle in the Haystack"

A family—two parents and their teenage daughter—was referred by Child Protective Services (CPS). They had sustained a number of hardships, including domestic violence, medical concerns, and substance abuse problems. The girl was reacting with academic problems and belligerence at home as a result. The family, however, only asked for one thing. They requested assistance to support an identified strength in their daughter that they had been unable to develop despite their best efforts. It was a simple request, really—the gift of piano lessons for a child whose parents and former teachers had observed budding musical talent.

This simple desire was made painfully difficult to fulfill due to the girl's special circumstances, however, for she was both blind and had a pervasive developmental disorder. It was no wonder the family had difficulty in finding a resource for their daughter, for community-based teachers with specialized skills needed to support such handicaps are few and expensive. Perhaps it would have been easier to find a needle in a haystack. Nevertheless, it was in support of this strength and the family's request that the CCSI program took on this mission. Literally 50 phone calls (and much research) later, they finally found a piano teacher who seemed promising. Was he available and willing, and could he deal with the child's handicaps?

Yes. In fact, he specialized in teaching blind students with Pervasive Development Disorder diagnoses. The staff was elated—for a moment—until the prospective teacher asked what kind of piano the child had; pointing out that practice was still required to develop musical interest no matter what the handicap. We learned from the family that, unfortunately, they had no piano and no resources to get one.

Back to the phones—another eight calls later and we talked to someone who was willing, after a description of the teen's more charming qualities, to donate a new piano to this personable young teen but only if we picked it up. A few calls later and we had secured the services of a company who was eager to deliver the piano and do it for free. Because of this success in supporting their singular request the family slowly began to trust us with more sensitive concerns, and we were able to eventually connect them to a variety of life-altering services, such as domestic violence counseling, drug treatment court, medical and vocational services

Clinical Vignette # 3: "The Skelton in the Meeting"

Sometimes you just need an entrée when working with a child or family. Referrals to the community services program usually are of people who have exhausted their own resources, tried every option and followed every lead they were given. These families when they arrive are frequently exhausted, disheartened and intensely discouraged—parents and children alike. If this is the case then creating meaningful dialogue about problems in a fresh way, or finding a way to tap into hidden resources, is the first challenge to master in renewing hope for a better future.

We are reminded, for example, of a thirteen-year-old boy, whose family came to us through CPS. Among other (and numerous) problems the family faced, they had been dealing with the child's sexual trauma, history of incest and domestic violence. As we marshaled the many resources for the network meeting with the family, the CCSI Coordinator (Cristantiello) recalled the child's fascination with Halloween, and the shocks, scares and delights of the night. The child and I had discovered a mutual interest in masks and had talked at length about our experiences with them. The meeting was a large one—15 providers in a room with the boy and family. We tried to make everyone as comfortable as possible with the process, and took great pains to elicit interaction and verbal expression from the family members involved.

Just before the meeting I gave the boy the gift of a mask that I had made out of papier-mâché along with a cape, as follow-up to our previous talk, and then the meeting commenced. As it progressed everyone noticed the boy was obviously intimidated by the sheer number of adults and the seriousness of the process. I attempted to put him at ease, but was only able to get barely audible, simple answers to questions, and no spontaneous dialogue. From previous interactions I knew he was able to communicate with more richness and conviction, and that he had useful things to communicate to the group, but I wondered how I could assist him to tap into that strength. He was still clutching his mask and cape—a skeleton—and I asked him if he'd like to put them on, a suggestion he readily agreed to. "What would the skeleton like to say?" I asked, and he responded in his best deep scary voice. We took off from there! "Skeleton" answered questions and talked to all at length—mask and cape in place—with eagerness and spontaneity.

Clinical Vignette # 4: "The Electric Guitar"

A teenage girl was referred after the horror of witnessing her mother's murder. A year after the incident, when we first met her, she was having problems in school, was getting into arguments and other social difficulties, and was underachieving to a serious degree. She tried to cope with her trauma and grief through poetry, and, expressed the wish that she could set her words to music. In inquiring further we found that, more than anything, she wanted an electric guitar although she did not directly ask us for one. Instead, she listened and responded to several other services we offered her as a result of our assessment: a trauma and grief specialist, and our assistance in the upcoming Committee on Special Education (CSE) meeting.

Keeping her unspoken wish for the guitar in mind we kept our eyes and ears open. Our perseverance eventually led us to a long holiday line in a music store, where we patiently waited to inquire in person (often much more effective than phone solicitation) for the possibility of old unclaimed guitars left for repair, or an outright donation of an instrument. The store personnel listened to our story but could offer no assistance. However, a woman, waiting in line behind us, had overheard our exchange. She had a guitar with her and came to the store to trade it in for an upgrade for her own daughter. But on hearing our tale she resolved to offer it to us for our poetic teen. That she did, and on Christmas that year our aspiring songwriter got what may have been the first good surprise of her recent life. She continues to develop her musical talent with this gift and to transform her experiences, including her grief and pain, into expressive hope.

Clinical Vignette #5: "Swarming Wasps Create a Portal of Entry"

The Family Advocate and Coordinator (Cristantiello) made a home visit to a ten-year-old girl and her mother. She was referred by the Persons in Need of Supervision (PINS) Diversion Team. She was caught in possession of marijuana and was in danger of being removed from the home because her mother worked 7 days a week and the child was unsupervised for long hours each day.

I (Cristantiello) met with her on the front steps on a warm summer day while the Family Advocate interviewed her mother inside the house. Her eyes were downcast and remarks monosyllabic for a good 20 minutes. I began to doubt whether we would make a personal connection. I diverted my gaze from this depressed, mosquito-bitten little girl and began to scan the property, giving her a break from my focused attentions and affording myself a chance to regroup. As I surveyed the view, I became aware of some hovering wasps that we both had only peripherally noted before. The wasps were going in and out of a small hole in the front step railing. We watched as a returning wasp touched the head of a wasp waiting to depart from the opening. The waiting wasp took off and returned to do the same thing to the next wasp. We began to muse over the meaning of this ritual and what one could see if you took the time to observe things closely. The girl had a

Photo of Bee

tender patience, keen perceptiveness and tolerance for what many would consider annoying pests. She was surprised at my willingness to stray from "business" and she began talking in full sentences. To encourage this budding connection I jumped up to retrieve my digital camera from the car and returned to take a close-up photo of the wasps. I showed her how to use the camera and waved her on to take her best shot, keeping an eye on the wasps. She moved along the property taking several pictures, and then showed them to me. This opened the floodgates of communication about disappointments, trauma, and loneliness.

When her mother came out she was surprised and pleased to find her daughter fully engaged. They had been isolated from one another for some time, each by their own depression, and were the worse for being cut off from the gifts each had to share. We printed her photos and had them framed and waiting for her weeks later at her Network Meeting. A room full of health care providers admired her artistry, and gained instant insight into her interests. They were introduced to this child not by her misdemeanors, not by her illness but by her evident spark and by her success. They were eager to find other ways to engage her intellect and talents and perhaps even put aside any pre-formed notions of the difficulties they thought they'd be faced with at the meeting this day.

Clinical Vignette #6: "The Artist in Hiding"

Sometimes children view themselves as "psychiatric disaster" cases. Usually when that is the case, someone else views them that way as well, often one or both parents, if not the whole family. Once children buy into this self-portrayal it can become entrenched and hard to change. A good example of this mislabeling is a girl we will call Kelly, 12 years old when treatment was initiated. Kelly attended a private day school, is bright, a child of varied interests, and talents, but she was primarily known in her family for her unrelenting fears and constant anxiety. The range of her fears was comprehensive and imaginative. Kelly worried about nuclear Armageddon, as well as toxicity in the environment that indeed we should all worry about but for her these fears were crippling. Kelly's rate of production of new fears while conquering old ones led her family to view her as headed for a lifetime of therapy.

Kelly always did her homework. Whenever she introduced a new fear in her sessions, for example cancer, she came fully prepared to discuss it in great depth, the many forms of cancers, the ones that existed in her family going back for multiple generations even if the occurrence was infrequent and all the variations of these forms of cancers, the gaps in current knowledge in treating the various cancers, the statistics on outcomes for the various forms of treatments, and all the theories of etiology that were currently in vogue plus a few of her own that were argued so logically they appeared quite plausible.

It was quite an education for the therapist (Crenshaw) as Kelly applied her high level of intelligence and strong work ethic to researching the latest of her obsessive worries and fears. She was particularly knowledgeable about the environmental toxins absorbed in the human body for which there are tests available to determine presence or absence. Clearly, Kelly's fears were not irrational, totally "off the wall" concerns; the crux of her suffering was due to the degree she fixated on and obsessed about these fears thereby constraining and limiting her life. She often refused to go with the family for meals in restaurants for fear of deficient sanitary conditions in the eating establishments; she restricted her social life to inviting occasionally just one or two friends to her house on a weekend, but never accepted invitations to their houses.

In family sessions, it was quickly revealed that Kelly had stiff competition for the distinction of suffering the greatest variety of fears. Her dad was a close rival. Her mother, by contrast was a confident and capable person, a prolific and highly admired college professor, chair of her academic department—she had little patience with either her husband or her daughter as they dueled to win the crown of the most impaired. The father, although a trained Certified Public Accountant, basically was sidelined by his never-ending fears and worries and worked infrequently.

While Kelly and her father, who frequently brought her to the sessions, were largely interested in talking about Kelly's latest research on emerging threats to our health or toxicity to the environment, I began to inquire in a determined way about her other interests, talents, and strengths. In the process of this exploration it turned out that Kelly was a gifted artist "in hiding"—in the sense that neither Kelly nor her father gave much attention or credence to her talent. Her mother was the exception as she recognized Kelly's talent and encouraged her in her artistic creations. Kelly was particularly gifted at watercolors and when the therapist finally convinced her to bring in some of her paintings he was amazed and awed at her gift.

When the focus shifted from Kelly as a "bundle of pathology" to a talented youngster who had an exceptional gift a different child emerged in the subsequent sessions. No longer preoccupied with her fears and worries, she reached the point where she had little interest in discussing them. It became clear that Kelly, out of loyalty to her father had closely identified with him. She feared relinquishing her obsessive fears and moving ahead in life because it felt disloyal, like she was leaving her father behind. It took persistent encouragement and persuasion but finally her father agreed to see a therapist himself regarding his chronic anxiety, fears, and phobias thus freeing Kelly to move on in her development. Shortly thereafter Kelly was ready to discontinue treatment as she no longer organized her life around her fearful preoccupations.

Kelly began to put her redirected energies into developing and nurturing her artistic talents and entered a number of art competitions and her success validated her rare and unusual talent. No one would suspect that this enthusiastic and talented youngster just a few months before was regarded as nearly hopelessly mired in her bundle of fears and worries. Kelly, herself, had nearly lost hope of ever living a normal life.

BREAKING THE CHAIN OF CHRONICITY WITH THE STRENGTHS-BASED APPROACH

One of the dangers of today's emphasis in psychiatry on classifying mental health problems according to a medical model of delineating pathology and prescribing psychopharmacological treatments is that it can be extremely disempowering to patients and their families. Once the child enters the mental health system parents may feel their child is in the hands of the "experts" and the parents will not know what to do. This invalidates the parents who often feel they are "out of their league" and only the experts can help their child. Once the child receives an official DSM-IV classification and perhaps some pharmaceuticals to alleviate the condition, the child and family are well along the way to feeling that the well-being and health of the child is in the hands of the mental health experts. We do not dispute that psychopharmacology has a legitimate and well-established role in the treatment of psychiatric disorders and that numerous adults and children receive benefit from them. These particular "side effects," however, are not often considered.

The strengths-based approach is a refreshing alternative to the pathology mind-set based on the medical model. In DSM-IV, there is not one page devoted to strengths, or assets of a person, rather page after page of systematic classification of a tremendous range of pathology, grouped into a plethora of disorders. We do not take the extreme position that there is no value in a diagnostic classification system such as DSM-IV. At times an accurate diagnosis can guide treatment interventions and lead to improved treatment results. It may be critically important in the evaluation and treatment of certain acute conditions, for example, drug-induced psychosis.

It is our contention, however, that an overinvestment in classification can impede treatment and demoralize patients and families. The late psychoanalyst, Walter Bonime (1989), maintained that nosology tended to obscure rather than illuminate the person. We do not advocate ignoring the existing pathology in the person but to pay as much attention to the health, strengths, and resources that exist in a person along with the features of impairment. Our clinical experience demonstrates change is augmented when you give equal weight to both the strengths and the pathological.

This chapter illustrates through brief clinical vignettes how a strengths-based approach to treatment can change the direction in a treatment process mired down in an over-focus on pathology. Most mental health professionals received their training in pathology-oriented models that cannot only be disempowering to our clients but can trap the therapist in an overwhelming sense of hopelessness. The same clinical case can be viewed as impossible because of the multitude of problems or alternatively viewed as offering numerous opportunities for us to help. It all depends on the mindset adopted.

In the Coordinated Children's Services Initiative, tending to the seemingly less significant requests of the children and families we serve often leads to the most powerful movement in this process. They acknowledge that we *do* hear even the smallest voice, they provide a point of connection that is low-stress and sometimes even playful and they provide an opportunity for families to test our credibility with less serious matters before entrusting us with their greatest concerns.

The strengths-based interventions discussed in the vignettes create a "portal of entry" with a child, teen, or family that facilitates hope, trust, and empathy. Such interventions can restart therapy when it has bogged down, or jump-start it when it is stalled at the beginning. At its core, this approach to therapy validates strengths and resources in the client rather than teaching them reliance on "experts" who supposedly will have the answers to their complex problems. It shows appreciation for the complexity of human development, and a healthy respect for the person, who is more than a bundle of pathology—far, far more.

REFERENCES

Bonime, W. (1989). *Collaborative psychoanalysis: Anxiety, depression, dreams, and personality change.* Rutherford, NJ: Fairleigh Dickinson University Press.

Brooks, R. (1993). *The search for islands of competence.* Presentation at the Fifth Annual Conference of CHADD. San Diego: CA.

Brooks, R. (2003). *Facilitating hope and resilience in children.* Keynote presentation at the Fiftieth Anniversary Conference of the Astor Home for Children. Fishkill, NY.

Brooks, R., and Goldstein, S. (2004). *Raising resilient children: Fostering strength, hope, and optimism in your child.* New York: McGraw-Hill.

Currie, E. (2004). *The road to whatever: Middle-Class culture and the crisis of adolescence.* New York: Metropolitan Book.

Merriam, K. (2006). *Searching for connection: An exploration of trauma, culture, and hope.* San Luis Obispo, CA: Truthsayer Press.

Minuchin, S., & Nichols, M. P. (1993). *Family healing: Tales of hope and renewal from family therapy.* New York: The Free Press.

Tebes, J. K., Feinn, R., Vanderploeg, J. J., Chinman, M. J., Shepard, J., Brabham, T., et al., (2007). Impact of a positive youth development program in urban after-school settings on the prevention of adolescent substance use. *Journal of Adolescent Health, 41,* 239–47.

Walsh, F. (2007). Traumatic loss and major disasters: Strengthening family and community resilience. *Family Process, 46,* 207–27.

Waters, D. B. & Lawrence, E. (1993). *Competence, courage and change: An approach to family therapy.* New York: Norton.

NOTE

1. This chapter is dedicated to Robert Brooks whose ground-breaking work on the strengths-based approach has injected a hopeful and energizing breath of fresh air into the rather dank, stark, and bleak theoretical climate with its emphasis on the pathological, so characteristic of traditional approaches to therapy.

6

The Hidden Dimensions: Unspeakable Sorrow and Buried Human Potential[1]

David A. Crenshaw and James Garbarino

OVERVIEW

Some of the most enraged kids encountered in clinical settings are youth who have been simply and narrowly judged as "bad kids" by many of the adults in their lives. But what may not be recognized is that most of these youngsters have suffered major and repeated losses, and in some cases traumatic losses (Garbarino, 1999). These losses were not honored, recognized by others, or grieved by the children. Nor did they receive support or facilitation of their grieving from the adults in their lives. This deep reservoir of unrequited sorrow is the smoldering emotional underbelly to their violence. Also in this deeper place in which the true essence of the child lives we find buried treasure, the untapped human potential and unrecognized redeeming qualities of these kids.

The metaphor of "fawns in gorilla suits" (Crenshaw & Hardy, 2005; Crenshaw & Mordock, 2005b) was introduced in previous writing to highlight some of the features of children in the foster care system who have suffered severe losses and for whom modifications in the empirically supported treatment protocols are needed in order to adequately and safely undertake therapeutic exploration of their traumatic grief.

CUMULATIVE LOSS AND BROKEN DREAMS

These children not only don't cry but they also don't dare to hope. Their dreams have been crushed too often. They can't bear further disappointments and broken promises. They adopt a survival orientation that keeps them focused on simply remaining alive for another day (Hardy, 2003). Many of them adopt a fatalistic worldview—"terminal thinking," as it is often called. When asked what they expect to be when 30, such kids may reply, "dead."

Many urban youth growing up in poor neighborhoods do not expect to live to see adult life and some have already planned their funerals in great detail. In their family the concern as to where the next meal is going to come from is a daily anxiety.

An African American father whose nine-year-old daughter had been shot in an urban neighborhood by a stray bullet expressed sadness that his daughter went from a child to an adult overnight. He explained that she used to be a typical child, carefree, full of energy but now appears sad and overburdened. Just prior to the shooting, the family had moved from a dangerous neighborhood to one that they thought would be safer.

The father went on to say that he calls home frequently when he is at work to make sure his family is okay. When stray bullets take down innocent children on their way to school or a family has to dive from their beds to the floor in the middle of the night to dodge stray bullets from a gunfight in the street, it is hard to adopt a positive view of the future.

An Early Encounter with a "Fawn in a Gorilla Suit"

Injuries to the spirit of a child are slow to heal; deep traumatic emotional wounds do not heal spontaneously. The wounds are deep and penetrate to the soul (Hardy, 2004, 2005a; Hardy & Laszloffy 2005). Emotionally wounded children have been exposed to some mix of economic oppression and domestic or neighborhood violence. Many have also suffered devaluation as a result of their race, class, gender, or sexual orientation. Some were born into families who tried to love and care for them but were overwhelmed with the oppressive burdens they faced. Many of these children are deeply sad, but may not be able to acknowledge this pain. Nor do the other people in their lives usually recognize it.

These are the kids we have been privileged to know during our careers and who have deeply touched our hearts. We came to think of them as "Fawns in Gorilla Suits," sensitive young souls trapped in the bodies of what many consider frighteningly powerful aggressors, although gorillas are actually the gentlest of the primates. Actually, the metaphor used to distinguish between outer and inner self of the violent child draws more from the Hollywood stereotype of men dressed in gorilla suits than the actual animal although it is true that once we peel away the layers and make a genuine connection with violent youth they don't seem so fierce either.

A fawn at the edge of the woods watches with a wary eye. Any sudden movement is likely to startle and send the fawn scurrying into the woods.

If, however, you don't signal aggression by approaching vigorously and directly but rather crouch down and be still, the fawn may cautiously move a step closer. Or as young fawns are prone to do they may lie perfectly still in the hope that potential predators don't see them. Children who are hurting deep inside from invisible but very real wounds are like fawns on the edge of the woods. They fear being hurt again. They don't dare approach because they won't be able to bear it if their hopes are crushed again. As much as they desire human contact, it will not be easy to convince them that it is available to them without unbearable cost.

These children never established basic trust, in an Eriksonian sense. They did not experience early in life the secure attachments that all children need to develop a sense of security, safety, and trust. They did not experience being cared for, loved, protected and nurtured. Some children do not get this at all; others receive it only unpredictably and inconsistently. The moments of nurture and love may be interspersed with anger or cold indifference. In some cases the quality of care the child received may have depended on whether the parent was sober or high at that moment.

The fawn protects the vulnerable, frightened core self by putting on the gorilla suit (aggression) to keep others at a safe distance. This ensures protection, at the cost of guaranteeing existential loneliness. Other deeply hurting children simply hide behind a brick wall of detachment like the fawn lying perfectly still in the grass, out of reach of emotional contact with anyone, no matter how genuinely caring and motivated to help the other person may be.

One child described in previous writing (Crenshaw & Mordock, 2005b) first seen more than 30 years ago stands out as an initial encounter with a "fawn in a gorilla suit." He was 11 years old. When the therapist's wife and young children came into the dining room to share dinner with the kids and staff of the residential treatment program, Miguel (fictitious name) would greet them at the door with a "smile that would melt butter" and usher them to the table. He would then make a fuss over them—run and fetch tea for the therapist's wife and milk for his two young daughters. He delivered both tea and milk with that unforgettable warm smile. Everyone knew Miguel was kindhearted and a good human being. Everyone in the program also knew that Miguel all too often donned the gorilla suit. Since he was a muscular, athletic youngster, he was capable in his rages of hurting others, even adult staff members.

One morning the therapist arrived at the program from the cottage his family occupied just inside the front gate of the treatment center. He drove slowly the one mile to the school building, dreading the profoundly sad and difficult task of telling Miguel that he had arranged for the social worker from his home state to take him back to be placed in a more secure treatment facility. The night before, Miguel had broken a chair over the heads of several of his dorm mates. A couple of those boys required stitches from the local hospital emergency room. This was the last in a series of violent episodes that posed serious risk to the other kids and the staff. The therapist brought Miguel into his office and delivered as sensitively as he could the message that the boy's dangerous behavior made it impossible to keep him and others safe in this setting.

As soon as he realized where this conversation was going Miguel darted out of the office and ran into the heavily wooded area surrounding the treatment center. The therapist pursued him and after a lengthy chase spotted him on a hill behind a big oak tree about 100 feet away. Not wanting to drive him further into the woods, the therapist stopped pursuing and called out to him, "Miguel you have to go back home." He immediately screamed back words that still pierce the heart today, "Don't you understand? This is my home! The only home I've ever had." Miguel did not have a home or a family to return to. He was in the custody of the Social Services department of his state and he was going to be placed in another facility, one that was more restrictive and less homelike.

After Miguel calmed down, he was willing to walk with the therapist back to the campus. The next day the therapist helped load his meager personal belongings in the state car in which his social worker had driven to campus to pick him up. Miguel did not look at the therapist. He just climbed in the front seat. The car started down the driveway but after only a few feet stopped. Miguel's door opened and he came rushing back. He gave the therapist an unforgettable heartrending hug. Neither the boy nor the therapist wanted to let go but eventually they did. As the therapist watched that car drive off, he felt a piece of his heart was headed out the front gate.

What happened to Miguel? Is he still alive? If the staff could have persisted just a little longer, might he have turned his life around? These questions will probably never be answered. But this much is clear: Miguel was our first encounter with a "fawn in a gorilla suit." Miguel taught us that if we can somehow get past the ugliness of violence, which we can never condone, what we will find is a frightened, vulnerable and all-too-often traumatized child who craves a "home for the heart" (Bettelheim, 1974). He also taught us that we can't do this work without our share of heartbreaking failures, no matter how hard we try.

Longing for What Never Was

When life provides children with secure attachments in their early development, they are privileged and fortunate. They are provided what the Irish poet John O'Donohue (2005) called "a shelter for the soul." Kids who begin life with secure attachments to the adults most important to them will tend to have a set of developmental assets that buffer them from the adversities that life presents. Children who are able to develop secure relationships with the people they love and who love them develop a solid foundation for the basis of self-identity and subsequent relationships. Secure attachments assist not only in reducing anxiety but also in helping to manage and regulate emotions (Siegel, 1999, Siegel and Hartzell, 2003).

Secure attachments predict the quality of future relationships to authority, when they become caregivers and care receivers as well (Bloom, 2002). Miguel was unfortunate. He did not experience in early life the secure attachments that form the foundation on which children learn basic trust. He did not receive this because in all probability his attachment figures did not receive it either in their early lives. They did not know how to provide for their own children what they had been deprived of in their own childhoods.

How many generations can this "psychological homelessness" (Hardy, 1997) be traced back, each succeeding generation needing that secure base of attachments that the previous generation missed out on and is unable to provide? Multiple generations of a family suffering from "psychological homelessness," never experiencing the "shelter for the soul," and relentlessly seeking and longing for a "home for the heart."

Disrupted early attachments frequently predispose children to destructive future relationships, impaired ability to regulate emotions, lack of close relationships, failure of empathy, problems in trusting others, and difficulties in relating to authority figures. They also increase risk for addictive behaviors and the risk for violence in relationships (Bloom, 2002; Siegel, 1999). In addition these attachment-deprived kids are at greater risk for failing to form secure attachments with their own children (Siegel and Hartzell, 2003). But the powerful underlying emotional force in those who miss out on what they desperately needed early in life is unresolved and buried grief. The aggression and violence seen in these youth often camouflage the profound underlying and neglected sorrow.

Traumatic Losses

The number of children in our inner cities who have experienced traumatic losses is staggering. The rate of homicide of young black youth, ages 15 to 19, is six times that of white youth of the same age and 20–50 times what it is for other youth the same age in other countries with modern democratic societies. In these high-crime dangerous neighborhoods it is not uncommon for young children to witness shootings, stabbings, and murders, including drive-by shootings. Imagine going to school and trying to focus on reading, writing, and spelling with the intrusive images of such violence flooding your mind. These children carry the deep sorrow and profound rage that accompanies the horrors that have been the steady diet of their daily lives. A study in one Chicago neighborhood found that 1 in 3 fifteen-year-olds had personally witnessed a homicide (Bell & Jenkins, 1993).

The School-Based Mourning Project: A Preventive Intervention in the Cycle of Inner-City Violence, conducted by Georgetown University Medical Center (Sklarew, Krupnick, Ward-Zimmer, & Napoli 2002) is a program focused on assisting children ages seven to fifteen to cope with multiples losses and trauma and to facilitate the work of mourning in these children. The project focuses on children who need this kind of intervention the most. The program was designed to take into account how difficult it is for inner-city children to confront their profound losses.

Living in chaotic, dangerous neighborhoods, extreme poverty, witnessing and suffering violence leaves kids little time or energy to grieve their losses. The authors state, "This inner-city war is most insidious. In contrast to normal warfare, in which the community coheres and acts as a group to fight the other, inner-city wars involve fighting within the community itself. While all wars are terrible and involve victimization, there is the expectation that some day it will be over. This is in striking contrast to the hopelessness in the inner city where the war continues, generation after generation" (Sklarew et al., 2002, p. 322; see also Cohen 1996).

In the inner city population treated by the child mourning project, many youth committed to prison or sent to residential treatment centers are fathers or fathers-to-be, whose absence will perpetuate the cycle of loss and violence in the children's lives. Harsh and punitive prison conditions become the fertile ground on which the seeds for further crime and violence are sown. The clinicians and researchers in this project describe these children as emotionally vulnerable and developmentally impaired, unable to cope with feelings of helplessness and hopelessness, the pain of grief, their own violent fantasies, and their ongoing sense of guilt, stigmatization, and shame. Often the youth try to avoid their underlying depression and unattended sorrow by aggressive acting-out or by self-destructive self-medicating behavior involving alcohol, drugs or sex. The clinicians work with the kids in a group format using a variety of projective methods, drawings, clay, games, stories, and musical instruments to structure the therapeutic setting and make it safe for children to acknowledge and express their grief. The techniques are similar to the ones described in previous writing (Crenshaw, 2004, 2005, 2006; Crenshaw & Mordock, 2005a) in that they rely on creative arts techniques and play therapy with the youngest children to enable them to safely undertake the grief and trauma work.

Due to the pervasive violence of the world we live in, many children suffer traumatic grief beyond those of the American inner city war zone. In a study of children and adolescents exposed to the military occupation of Kuwait that was the catalyst for the Gulf war, 70% reported moderate to severe post-traumatic stress reactions (Nader, Pynoos, Fairbanks, Al-Ajeel, et al. 1993). A recent study of post-traumatic stress in former Ugandan child soldiers found that 97% reported post-traumatic stress reactions of clinical significance (Derluyn, Broekaert, Schuyten, & Temmerman, 2004). Of the 301 former child soldiers interviewed, 77% witnessed someone being killed and 39% had to kill someone themselves. The authors report that worldwide, 300,000 children are currently used as child soldiers in armed conflicts.

Treatment of Childhood Traumatic Grief

Cohen and Mannarino (2004) tested a treatment model that addresses both grief and trauma symptoms. These clinicians and researchers have found that trauma symptoms impinge on the children's ability to undertake the normal grieving process. In the normal grieving process children are "able to access the person in memory in a manner that is positive and beneficial to integrating the death in his or her total life experience" (Cohen & Mannarino, 2004, p. 255). Their empirically derived treatment model includes a parental treatment component as well. They explain that children who experience traumatic grief are preoccupied with the traumatic circumstances of the death and the loss itself cannot be fully experienced and the pain of the grief cannot thereby diminish. In his pioneering work Pynoos (1992) identified three types of triggers to the intrusive and disturbing trauma related images, memories, and thoughts. Cohen and Mannarino built upon this when they wrote,

> Trauma reminders are situations, people, places, sights, smells, or sounds that remind the child of the traumatic nature of the death. For example, tall buildings or hearing airplanes overhead may be trauma reminders for children whose parents died in the September 11th terrorist attacks. Loss reminders are people, places, objects, situations, thoughts, or memories that remind the child of the deceased loved one. A parent's birthday or seeing pictures of their deceased parents may be loss reminders for these children. Change reminders are situations, people, places, or things that remind the child of changes in living circumstances caused by the traumatic death. (Cohen & Mannarino, 2004, p. 820)

Having to change schools or no longer having their older brother who was killed in a drive-by shooting to walk them to school may be change reminders for these children.

The treatment model is used for children ages 6 to 17 who have significant child traumatic grief symptoms. Although the treatment is manualized, the authors recognize that therapist creativity and flexibility are critical ingredients for effective implementation. The treatment protocol consists of separate individual treatment for the parent and child in 8–12 sessions while 4 additional sessions are reserved for joint parent-child treatment. Specific components of the treatment model are trauma-focused and grief-focused. A detailed analysis of each of these components is beyond the scope of this paper but interested readers are urged to read the original article by Cohen and Mannarino (2004).

Suggested Modification of the Model for "Fawns in Gorilla Suits"

The CTG treatment model above has gained empirical support as a relatively short-term intervention with children who have experienced traumatic loss. In our judgment, modifications are needed for those diagnosed as Conduct Disorder, kids whose lives are often replete with trauma and loss (Greenwald, 2002), who are eventually placed in either residential treatment centers or the juvenile justice system. Because of the cumulative losses and the dehumanized response to their losses, as well as the severity of the trauma and violence exposure, these children and youth will require a more extensive individual and/or family therapy approach that gradually builds strong enough therapeutic alliances to allow the youth to confront the traumatic events at their own pace, cautiously and safely. Cohen and Mannarino (2004) are astute clinicians and recognize that the two to three sessions allotted in the manualized protocol for creating the trauma narrative would not be realistic for treatment with youngsters whose losses are unspeakable.

When Lenore Terr (1983) conducted a 4-year follow-up study of 25 children who had been kidnapped and buried underground for 48 hours, every child exhibited posttraumatic effects. She concluded that brief treatment 5–23 months after the kidnapping did not prevent trauma symptoms 4 years later. Furthermore, she found that symptom severity was related to prior vulnerabilities, family pathology, and level of community support. Thus short-term treatments, even in the case of single-event trauma, are not always adequate when the trauma event is horrific. For children who have extensive prior loss histories and other risk factors, the need for more extensive treatment will be especially compelling. In addition, due to the disorganizing effects of anxiety associated with the original terror of these events, many of these youngsters will need more indirect work using the safe haven of symbol and metaphor to work up to direct confrontation with the traumatic losses to avoid flooding and the risk of re-traumatization (Crenshaw, 2005).

The Cohen and Mannarino model also included a parent treatment component and the impact of trauma on the child's family cannot be ignored (Hardy, 2005b). The family offers powerful resources for healing but may be a therapeutic impediment as well. The family dynamics may be either enlisted in trauma recovery or may present a formidable barrier if ignored.

Families may be insistent on not discussing the trauma events for fear of making the situation worse or overwhelming for individual family members or the family as a whole.

Other families may insist on children talking about the events before they are prepared to do so in a therapeutic manner. The family treatment component should include a psychoeducational focus to educate families about the typical symptoms of trauma, and the stages of trauma recovery. Family members can be recruited to help in providing soothing and calming responses to the traumatized family member and when needed to set limits. The family can also be educated regarding the typical pitfalls that families encounter in the trauma healing process including the demoralizing response from others of "enough already" (Hardy, 2005b).

Crucial to success in reclaiming our lost and despairing youth is a relentless pursuit of strengths, talents, and redeeming qualities, the "buried treasure" to be found in these kids. Hardy and Laszloffy (2005) urged clinicians to look for "badges of ability" in potentially violent youth; to delineate strengths and talents that the child can point to with pride. Nearly every youth has unclaimed potential. Opportunities for validation of one's skill, talent, and worth are readily available to those who grow up in affluent homes and communities, with favorable educational experiences. Those growing up in poor neighborhoods and poor rural areas have far less experiences of validation. When turning points are examined in the lives of youngsters who grew up under harsh circumstances, often they will cite an example of a person who would not give up on them or someone who saw something good in them when most could only see what was bad in them. The late Floyd Patterson, former heavyweight boxing champion, credited a former teacher with turning his life around when she went out of her way to show faith and confidence in him (Van Ornum & Mordock, 1983).

Another key therapeutic ingredient for those with losses beyond words is finding meaning in suffering. Victor Frankl emphasized that those with the deepest scars can potentially find the greatest depth of meaning (Barnes, 1994). Religious and spiritual teachings on this issue generally concur. For example, Buddhists and Jesuit Catholics emphasize the role of learning detachment through times of "consolation" and as a key step toward achieving internal harmony and peacefulness. The therapeutic task is to relate the experience of suffering to a meaning that the child and adolescent can accept. This is part of the task of creating a coherent and meaningful narrative that the interpersonal neurobiological approach has emphasized as crucial not only to mental well-being but to integration of the brain (Siegel, 2005).

A recent study, however, reported that among young adults, positive outcomes such as reduced fear of death and increased meaning in life are relatively rare in those who have been exposed to traumatic events (Floyd, Coulon, Yanez, & Lasota, 2005). It is not clear whether this was due to lack of therapeutic attention to this issue of meaning making or whether it relates to the "spiritual emptiness" of today's youth.

Many contemporary young people seen in clinical settings lack a sense of the world as having a meaningful, purposeful, or loving core. This spiritual emptiness leaves a "hole in the heart" of kids that they may be tempted to fill up by turning to the dark, destructive side of life. Spiritually empty kids can go into "free fall" rather quickly when the environment they live in begins to deteriorate (Garbarino, 2006). In other words, a sense of meaning, purpose, belief in a basically loving world, can buffer people spiritually in much the same way that secure attachments in early life get them off to a good start. Sadly, far too many kids miss out on both kinds of protective experiences and are left to cope alone in the universe, frightened fawns locked in gorilla suits for fear of confronting the terror of a traumatically meaningless world.

Empirical support for the crucial role of spiritual meaning comes from a recent study by Mascaro and Rosen (2006). They used an ethnically diverse sample of 143 college undergraduates to test the hypothesis that a sense of existential meaning buffers against the effect of stress on depression and hope. Mascaro and Rosen found that spiritual meaning as measured by the Spiritual Meaning Scale and personal meaning as measured by the framework subscale from the Life Regard Index-Revised were significantly negatively correlated with depressive symptoms and positively correlated with hope. Further, Mascaro and Rosen reported that spiritual meaning, but not personal meaning, moderated the relationship between stress and depression such that there was a strong relationship between depression and stress for individuals with low levels of spiritual meaning but no relationship between stress and depression for individuals with high levels of spiritual meaning. These investigators summarized their findings by stating that though both spiritual and personal meaning are inversely related to depression and positively related to hope, only spiritual meaning moderates the relationship between daily stress and depression.

The problem of youth violence will not be solved until we fully acknowledge the ambivalent relationship with violence so clearly seen in our culture and in ourselves. We denounce it, deplore it, yet we are fascinated and mesmerized by violence. The problem is not likely to significantly improve until we as a society, and we as individuals face the sobering truth that what is seen on the wide screen (of culture) is merely the projection of what exists within each of us.

The work of Stephen Diamond (1996) explored the psychology of evil building on the earlier work of Rollo May (1969) as well as others whom he cites such as Freud, Carl Jung, Erich Fromm, Bruno Bettelheim, Viktor Frankl, Karl Menninger, Robert Lifton, and more recently Peck (1983). Diamond notes that we have turned a blind eye to evil for so long that we can barely recognize let alone understand it. Diamond cites Rollo May's use of the classical Greek idea of the daimon to provide the basis for his mythological model of the *daimonic*. "The daimonic is any natural function which has the power to take over the whole person" (May, 1969, p. 123). Diamond emphatically stated that hostility, hatred, and violence are the greatest evils we have to contend with today and that evil has always been with us and will remain an existential reality that we as humans must come to honestly face. Unless we as potential healers come face to face with our potential for hatred, evil, and violence we will not be able to be fully effective as healers to violent youth. Diamond emphasizes the need for intensive emotionally focused work in working through the emotional wounds and traumatic reactivity in order to find meaning and purpose or spiritual renewal.

The road to healing of violent youth does not afford short cuts or quick fixes. It requires courage and perseverance on the part of the child and the healer. It requires staying the course in the turbulent waters of profound sorrow and intense rage. At many points there may be the temptation to turn back and return to shore by both child and healer but reaching the other side and discovering that such troubled waters can be crossed and survived leads to not only a fuller access to human potentials in the child but a validation of all that draws a healer to this work and greater confidence in our clinical skills.

REFERENCES

Barnes, R. C. (1994). Finding meaning in unavoidable suffering. *International Forum for Logotherapy, 17,* 20–26.

Bell, C., & Jenkins, E. J. (1993). Community violence and children on Chicago's Southside. *Psychiatry, 56,* 46–54.

Bettelheim, B. (1974). *A home for the heart.* New York: Alfred Knopf.

Bloom, S. L. (2002). Beyond the beveled mirror: Mourning and recovery from childhood maltreatment. In J. Kauffman (Ed.), *Loss of the Assumptive World* (pp. 139–70). New York: Brunner-Routledge.

Cohen, D. (1996). *Praeger Lecture.* George Washington University, Department of Psychiatry.

Cohen, J. A., & Mannarino, A. P. (2004). Treatment of childhood traumatic grief. *Journal of Clinical Child and Adolescent Psychology, 33,* 819–31.

Crenshaw, D. A. (2004). *Engaging resistant children in therapy: Projective drawing and storytelling strategies.* Rhinebeck, NY: Rhinebeck Child and Family Center Publications.

Crenshaw, D. A. (2005). Clinical tools to facilitate treatment of childhood traumatic grief. *Omega: Journal of Death and Dying, 51,* 239–55.

Crenshaw, D. A. (2006). *Evocative strategies in child and adolescent psychotherapy.* Lanham, MD: Jason Aronson.

Crenshaw, D. A., & Hardy, K. V. (2005). Understanding and treating the aggression of traumatized children in out-of-home care. In N. B. Webb (Ed.), *Working with traumatized youth in child welfare* (pp. 171-95). New York: Guilford Press.

Crenshaw, D. A., & Mordock, J. B. (2005a). *A handbook of play therapy with aggressive children.* Lanham, MD: Jason Aronson.

Crenshaw, D. A., & Mordock, J. B. (2005b). *Understanding and treating the aggression of children: Fawns in gorilla suits.* Lanham, MD: Jason Aronson.

Derluyn, I., Broekaert, E., Schuyten, G., & Temmerman, E. D. (2004). Post-traumatic stress in former Ugandan child soldiers. *Lancet, 363,* 861-63.

Diamond, S. A. (1996). *Anger, madness, and the daimonic.* Albany: State University of New York Press.

Floyd, M., Coulon, C., Yanez, A. P., & Lasota, M. T. (2005). The existential effects of traumatic experiences: A survey of young adults. *Death Studies, 29,* 55-63.

Garbarino, J. (1999). *Lost boys: Why our sons turn violent and how we can save them.* New York: Anchor Books.

Garbarino, J. (2006). Words can hurt forever. *Dan Kirk Memorial Lecture,* March 22, 2006. Marist College, Poughkeepsie, New York.

Greenwald, R. (2002). The role of trauma in conduct disorder. *Journal of Aggression, Maltreatment and Trauma,* 6, 2002, 5-23.

Hardy, K. V. (1997). Not quite home: The psychological effects of oppression. *The Family,* January, 7-8, 26.

Hardy, K. V. (2003). *Working with aggressive and violent youth.* Presentation at the Psychotherapy Networker Symposium, March 21st 2003. Washington, DC.

Hardy, K. V. (2004). *Getting through to violent kids.* Presentation at the Psychotherapy Networker Symposium, March 6, 2004. Washington, DC.

Hardy, K. V. (2005a). *Death before dis': Therapy with African American youth.* Presentation at Psychotherapy Networker Symposium, March 19th 2005. Washington, DC.

Hardy, K. V. (2005b). *Trauma treatment in context: A relational approach.* Presentation at the Psychotherapy Networker Symposium, March 18, 2005. Washington, DC.

Hardy, K. V., & Laszloffy, T. A. (2005). *Teens who hurt: Clinical interventions to break the cycle of adolescent violence.* New York: Guilford Press.

Mascaro, N., & Rosen, D. H. (2006). The role of existential meaning as a buffer against stress. *Journal of Humanistic Psychology, 46,* 168-90.

May, R. (1969). *Love and will.* New York: Norton.

Nader, K., Pynoos, R. S., Fairbanks, L. A., Al-Ajeel, M., et al. (1993). A preliminary study of PTSD and grief among the children of Kuwait following the Gulf crisis. *British Journal of Clinical Psychology, 32,* 407-16.

O'Donohue, J. (1999). *Anam Cara: Spiritual wisdom form the Celtic world.* New York: Bantam.

O'Donohue, J. (2005). *Awakening the imagination.* Presentation at the Psychotherapy Networker Symposium, March 17, 2005. Washington, DC.

Peck, S. M. (1983). *People of the Lie: The Hope for Healing Human Evil.* New York: Simon and Schuster.

Pynoos, R. S. (1992). Grief and trauma in children and adolescents. *Bereavement Care, 11,* 2-10.

Siegel, D. (1999). *The developing mind: How relationships and the brain interact to shape who we are.* New York: Guilford Press.

Siegel, D. (2005). *Psychotherapy and the integration of consciousness.* Presentation at the Psychotherapy Networker Symposium, March 20, 2005. Washington, DC.

Siegel, D., & Hartzell, M. (2003). *Parenting from the inside out.* New York: Jeremy P. Tarcher/Penquin.

Sklarew, B., Krupnick, J., Ward-Zimmer, D., & Napoli, C. (2002). The School-based mourning project: A preventive intervention in the cycle of inner-city violence. *Journal of Applied Psychoanalytic Studies, 4,* 317–30.

Terr, L. C. (1983). Chowchilla revisited: The effects of psychic trauma four years after a school-bus kidnapping. *American Journal of Psychiatry, 140,* 1543–150.

Van Ornum, W., & Mordock, J. B. (1983). *Crisis counseling with children.* New York: Continuum.

NOTE

1. An earlier version of this chapter was published in the *Journal of Humanistic Psychology,* Vol. 47 No. 2, April 2007, DOI: 10.1177/0022167806293310 ©Sage Publications and is reprinted with permission.

7

When Grief Is a Luxury Children Can't Afford

David A. Crenshaw and Linda Hill

There is no grief like the grief that does not speak.

—Henry Wordsworth Longfellow

The deeper the sorrow the less tongue it hath.

—The Talmud

My grief lies all within, and these external manners of lament are merely shadows to the unseen grief that swells with silence in the tortured soul.

—William Shakespeare

OVERVIEW

In large-scale disasters, or under conditions of war, grief is a luxury because survival depends on the carrying out of the mission or performing the duties that are thrust on survivors under these unimaginable conditions. Cultural factors play a role as well because some parts of the world are beset with such horrible conditions, like famine, disease, and abject poverty that death is viewed as a relief from intolerable suffering. In addition, children may not be able to afford the luxury of grief for multiple reasons that will be explored in this chapter including the overwhelming nature of the losses, the lack of sufficient internal resources to undertake the grief process, and/or the denial of sufficient external supports or even sanction to grieve.

The gifted writer, Goldberry Long (2007), author of *Juniper Tree Burning* (2001), discussed in an essay "time" that is demarcated by a past that preceded a devastating loss and a future where the loss will always be an unfailing presence. Another masterful writer, Joan Didion (2005) in eloquent prose described that division of time before the untimely and unexpected death of her husband and the year following. In many ways her world as she knew it came to a jolting stop and she described the painful, agonizing process of trying to restart it. But what of the people, especially children, who don't have the luxury to pause, to reflect on memories, feelings, to attend to their grief, to honor and commemorate the life of their loved one?

After the inconceivable loss of lives following the tsunami in Southeast Asia, Tunku Varadarajan, a features editor for the Wall Street Journal, wrote a thought provoking piece called, "How to Read the New Portraits of Grief: Individualism and Death in Southeast Asia" (*Wall Street Journal,* January 7, 2005). Varadarajan observed that most of the people who lost their lives, their homes, or their livelihood in the tsunami were destitute, and to be poor in their parts of the world means that you both live and die in anonymity.

Varadarajan noted the cruel irony that as a consequence of mass obliteration the stories of small farmers and fishermen living in the shadows and obscurity imposed by abject poverty were suddenly featured in stories in newspapers around the world. Briefly, as a result of this unspeakable tragedy, some of the anonymous were given names and faces.

The catastrophe was so immense that the stories of most of the 230,000 people swept into the sea insured that their deaths were accorded the same anonymity that characterized their lives. In such disasters, or in parts of Africa, such as Zambia where malaria claims the lives of countless infants and numerous AIDS related deaths occur, grief is a luxury that few can afford.

WHEN CHILDREN CAN'T AFFORD THE LUXURY OF GRIEF

In a UNICEF report (Bellamy, 2005) titled "Childhood under Threat," the shocking picture emerged of the conditions faced by countless children at the beginning of the 21st century. Among the startling findings of the UNICEF report were the following:

1) Of the two billion children living in the world, 1 billion are living in poverty.
2) 640 million children live without adequate shelter.
3) 400 million children have no access to safe drinking water.
4) The daily death toll of children under age 5 is 29,158.
5) The number of children who have been orphaned by the AIDS epidemic worldwide is 15 million.

The Denial of Childhood

Children who grow up in abject poverty, deprived of safe drinking water, adequate nutrition, denied adequate education or medical care, miss out on the most basic ingredients of childhood as viewed in developed countries. Add to these basic privation, kidnappings by paramilitary groups in nations torn by armed conflict, the coercing of children into combat or sexual slavery and the picture of childhood that many in the developed world take for granted becomes a grim and horrifying nightmare. In such environments, the grief of an individual child or family would garner little attention in relation to the enormity of the catastrophe, and not only because of the overwhelming nature of the conditions but grieving would distract from the daily ongoing tasks that survival hinges on.

Even in the developed world there are far too many children who do not experience the protected childhood that every child deserves, a time to grow, play, and develop in a surrounding environment that is reasonably predictable and safe. Children growing up in families and regions faced with a day-to-day struggle just to survive are not only deprived of a childhood but can't even afford the luxury to grieve their lost childhood.

Emotional Resources Denied to Children

Children can't always afford the luxury of grief because they have not developed fully the emotional resources required to reflect on and process grief both cognitively and emotionally. They may cope by distraction, denying the impact of the distressing life events or even acting-out in some disturbing way because they can't tolerate the emotional distress of grief.

Children don't have the luxury of grief because they fear being overwhelmed—swept away in a tidal way of grief. They may believe that if they give expression to their tears they will never stop crying. This inhibition against embracing the pain of grief leads to misunderstandings in the family when one child grieves openly while another only wants to go play ball with his friends. The child who seems cold and indifferent is typically a child who can't bear feeling the full force of grief and desperately is looking for ways to distract from the pain. They simply don't have yet the psychological resources to undertake the arduous process of grief.

Social Supports Denied to Children

Far too often, children lack adequate support or in some cases sanction to grieve. Ken Doka (1989, 2002) introduced the concept of *disenfranchised grief* that delineated grief related to unrecognized losses or losses associated with stigma such as suicide or death related to commission of a crime, for example, that receive little or no support from the community. The grief is not recognized, not sanctioned, and its expression may even be met with disapproval. This concept has been applied to children as well (Crenshaw, 2002). One of the most frequent examples of disenfranchised grief in children is the profound sorrow that many children experience when a family pet dies. Adults sometimes minimize or even trivialize such a loss regarding the pet merely as a "critter." The meaning of the death to the child is ignored or not understood. Nor is it appreciated that for many children this is the child's first meaningful encounter with death.

Children in the foster care system are frequently moved about from foster home to foster home perhaps eventually ending up in a group care facility. Along the way they suffer numerous broken relationships some of which may have been significant attachments. Often, little sensitivity is shown to children in the child welfare system to the cumulative losses they have experienced, particularly in terms of their meaning and significance for that particular child. As a result these children receive the message that their losses are not of interest, they are devalued and trivialized and the children themselves may view them as unimportant while the cumulative grief grows and is buried deeper. These children learned a long time ago it does no good to cry. Their tears are not acknowledged by others and eventually themselves. They simply don't have the luxury to grieve.

In addition the grief of many young children is disenfranchised because their well-meaning parents or caregivers decide that the children are too young to understand that their mom or dad has died. The younger the child when a parent dies the more likely it is to be traumatic, particularly for children 5 and under (Lieberman, Compton, Van Horn, & Ippen, 2003). Yet these are the children who so often are viewed as "simply too young to understand." They may be given less information and support than older children even though the loss impacts them in a more direct and devastating way because they are so young and dependent on the parent who died as well as the surviving parent. We sometimes marvel that a young child sometimes receives more emotional preparation for visiting the pediatrician to receive a shot than they do when a parent dies. The well-meaning parents often simply don't know what to say or they may find it emotionally too painful to address the loss with such a young child. Also, of course, the surviving parent is caught in the throes of their own acute grief.

For the above reasons, a series of stories called the "Bramley Story Series" were written to be used in therapy to assist not only the preschool child but the parents of such children when an important family loss occurs (Crenshaw, 2006b). The goal of the story series is to open up communication between the parent(s) and the preschool children in developmentally appropriate language and to establish the important principle that the child can talk with their parent at any age when questions, feelings, or memories arise. Otherwise, the unspeakable death may become a formidable barrier in the relationship between surviving parent(s) and child.

The Law of Grief

David Epston (White & Epston, 1990), a family therapist in New Zealand known for the narrative approach to therapy, wrote a letter to a fifteen-year-old boy who eleven months before was involved in a car accident that claimed the lives of his beloved older brothers, 19 and 17 years old. In the letter, Epston wrote:

> But remember the law of grief: Crying on the outside means that you are no longer crying on the inside. And crying on the inside drowns your strength. (White and Epston, 1990, p. 103)

This eloquently stated "law of grief" aptly points to the compelling value of expressing the multitude of tears that accompany life's most painful and inevitable losses. But what if no one is receptive? What if it is not considered appropriate and right to cry? What if the culture regards the tears of a male child as unmanly? What happens if the tears make the pain of your parents or siblings unbearable? What if you don't have the luxury to attend to your enormous sadness or to express the tears within, because your daily life is consumed with the struggle to survive? What if one devastating loss is followed by another and then another? What if some of the losses are so overwhelming it is too painful to focus on them and yet memories and intrusive thoughts flood the mind of the child while in school trying to do work? What if the child can't sleep at night due to reliving the drive-by shooting of a brother that was witnessed in a horrifying moment, vividly etched forever in the bereaved child's mind? Where do these unexpressed tears, the unattended sorrow, go? In extreme cases it injures the spirit and scars the soul of a child. A Biblical passage expressed the anguish that accompanies such wounds, "A man's spirit sustains him in sickness, but a crushed spirit who can bear?" (Proverbs 18:14).

The child and family may be unable to attend to their grief because it would make them too vulnerable and threaten their orientation to survival (Crenshaw & Hardy, 2005; Hardy & Laszloffy, 2005).You can't afford the luxury of grief if your survival is threatened. If your very existence is at stake every day, survival becomes your total preoccupation.

THERAPEUTIC FACILITATION OF GRIEF IN CHILDREN WHO CAN'T AFFORD TO GRIEVE

How do we access in a therapeutic way buried grief in youngsters whose life stories contain far too much horror and trauma. A model for treating childhood traumatic grief building on the ground-breaking work of Judith Cohen and Anthony Mannarino (2004; see also Cohen, Goodman, Brown, & Mannarino, A. 2004; Cohen, Mannarino, & Deblinger, 2006; Cohen, Mannarino, & Knudsen, 2004; Cohen, Mannarino, & Staron, 2006;) was previously proposed (Crenshaw, 2007). Cohen and Mannarino are cutting edge researchers and clinicians who have been exceptionally sensitive to the problems of implementing research protocols into daily clinical practice. They are among a seminal group of clinicians that include Alan Kazdin (Goodheart, Kazdin, & Sternberg, 2006; Kazdin, 2005a, 2005b), John Weisz (Weisz, 2004; Weisz & Addis, 2006), and Edna Foa (Cook, Schnurr, & Foa, 2004; Foa, Cahill, & Pontoski, 2004), who are trying to construct a bridge of realistic implementation from empirical research protocols to the world of clinical practice. They are unusually open to the problems of clinicians in the treatment of patients in a wide range of settings and with a complex array of clinical conditions. These cutting edge clinicians and researchers are also unusually flexible in being willing to modify and adapt the research protocols when required by the needs of patients.

The expanded model (Crenshaw, 2007) is also informed by recent interpersonal neurobiological and attachment theory research (Perry, 2005; Schore, 2003a, Schore, 2003b; Siegel, 1999). This research places great importance on establishing safety in the therapeutic relationship that enables children to face emotional states that would otherwise overwhelm or retraumatize; to repair disrupted memory systems, including the recovery and preservation of positive memories (Cohen & Mannarino, 2004; Cohen, Mannarino, & Deblinger, 2006) that without empathic intervention can become inaccessible—a harrowing loss; and to find meaning as well as create a coherent narrative. Twelve essential tasks of grieving to address traumatic loss were identified:

1) Create a Sense of Safety
2) Acknowledge the Reality of Losses
3) Identify, Embrace, and Express the Emotions of Grief
4) Commemorate the Losses
5) Acknowledge Ambivalence
6) Resolve the Ambivalence
7) Recover and Preserve Positive Memories
8) Honor the Timeless Attachments
9) Find and Create a Coherent Narrative
10) Let Go
11) Move On
12) Plan a Therapeutic Termination

After a brief review of the concept of childhood traumatic grief, five of the above tasks of grieving that are particularly relevant to children who don't have the luxury to grieve due to the overwhelming nature of the losses will be discussed.

Childhood Traumatic Grief

Cohen and Mannarino (2004) defined childhood traumatic grief (CTG) as a condition in which trauma symptoms interfere with the child's ability to negotiate the normal grieving process. Cohen and Mannarino described an empirically derived treatment model for CTG that addressed both trauma and grief symptoms and included a parental treatment component as well.

The interpersonal neurobiological approach as described by Daniel Siegel (1999; Siegel & Hartzell, 2003) and Allan Schore (2003a, 2003b) combines research findings from attachment research with neuroscience's discoveries of the way the brain develops. Kandel's (2005) work on neural plasticity, for which he received a Nobel Prize in the year 2000, stressed that the development and organization of the brain is experience-dependent. Bruce Perry (1997) stated, "There is no more specific 'biological' determinant than a relationship. Human beings evolved as social animals, and the majority of the biology of the brain is dedicated to mediating the complex interactions required to keep small, naked, weak, individual human beings alive by being part of a larger *biological* whole—the family, the clan. Indeed, it is the primary caretaking relationships of infancy and childhood that determine the core neurobiological organization of the human individual, thereby allowing this incredible social specialization. Early life experience determines core neurobiology" (p. 126).

In more recent writing Perry (2005) emphasized a neurosequential model of therapeutic intervention with child trauma. He stated, "The key to therapeutic intervention is to remember that the stress response systems originate in the brainstem and diencephalon. As long as these systems are poorly regulated and dysfunctional, they will disrupt and dysregulate the higher parts of the brain" (pp. 38–39). Perry further asserted, "All the best cognitive-behavioral, insight-oriented, or even affect-based interventions will fail if the brainstem is poorly regulated" (p. 39).

The consequences of unacknowledged and unresolved grief are persistent throughout life. Attachment researchers have found that unresolved grief and trauma reduces the flexibility of adults to access information about childhood and hampers their ability to reflect upon such information in a coherent manner and thereby reduces their likelihood of raising securely attached children (Siegel, 1999; Siegel & Hartzell, 2003). Grief is something you can't go around. You have to go through it in order to learn to live with it. If the mourning process is skipped, avoided or interrupted, the child is at risk for manifesting either delayed or distorted grief reactions. In delayed reactions, the bereaved child may show little or no outward signs of mourning at the time of a significant loss, only to react with profound grief at a later time in response to a loss of seeming less significance. In the case of distorted grief, again the bereaved child may show few signs of intense grief at the time of loss but later develop psychosomatic symptoms such as migraines, gastrointestinal symptoms or dizzy spells. They may become irritable and angry in their interpersonal relationships, sometimes leading to serious conflicts.

A major goal of therapy is to prevent subsequent psychopathology by assisting bereaved children to mourn their losses as fully as their developmental capacities allow (Webb, 2002). When children or unable to mourn the loss of loved ones due to the overwhelming or traumatic conditions of the loss, they are at risk for distorted or delayed grief reactions.

Key Therapeutic Tasks for Children Who Don't Have the Luxury to Grieve

Create a Safe Place

Safety is a precious commodity for children who rarely experience it. One of the essential ways that safety is created in the therapeutic setting is through the secure attachment formed with the therapist. Children, who live in a constant state of physiological hyperarousal, hypervigilant to threat, always scanning for signs of danger, can't easily imagine let alone find a safe place in this world. When asked to draw a picture of a safe place, many children who have suffered traumatic losses are unable to do so. Some may attempt to artistically create a safe place but then in the process their intended "safe place" becomes overrun with intruders and assailants. Their sense of trust and safety in the world has been shattered. Some engage in startle reactions at any sudden movement.

Children exposed to chronic violence will pay more attention in the classroom to the teacher's tone of voice, facial expressions, and other non-verbal communication than the words of the teacher. They've learned that survival in their unpredictable violent world depends more on accurate and quick readings of non-verbal cues than on verbal communication. It is necessary to make therapy with these youngsters not only a safe place, and build trust between the child and therapist, but to teach them self-calming and self-soothing skills to deal with their adrenaline and cortisol driven, always on-alert stress response systems. In Bruce Perry's terms, we need to help them learn to "soothe their brain stems."

These children are unable to soothe or calm themselves and their heart rates frequently reflect abnormal elevations even during sleep (Perry 1997; Perry & Szalavitz 2006). It is helpful to include in the beginning of the therapeutic session some form of calming and soothing activity, such as collaborative relaxation exercises, listening to music that calms or soothes the particular child, or selecting activities such as drawing that may have a calming effect on some children. If this is not done, the child may not be able to process the language of the therapist, because as the trauma researchers have demonstrated when the limbic system, particularly the amygdala is activated due to perceived threat, the higher cortical areas of the brain tend to go off line (Perry, 1997; van der Kolk, 2003).

Teaching self-soothing is further complicated by the fact that children may be able to process information at an age appropriate level when the topic is emotionally neutral but then lose their ability to track, focus, reason, process and express language, when the topic shifts to an emotionally charged issue. In the same session the cognitive, language, and emotional functioning of the child may vary widely depending on the degree of threat experienced by the activation of emotions and memories related to trauma or unresolved losses. Thus, therapists must be child responsive in their interventions sensitively and dynamically shifting when the level of threat makes the therapy context unsafe for the child.

Timing and pacing are two key factors that must be skillfully monitored by the therapist in response to cues given by the child. No child should be coerced or pressured into confronting painful, especially traumatic events, until they are ready (Perry & Szalavitz, 2006). The therapist can actively create opportunities for children to approach these events and use indirect methods such as play, metaphor, story, and drawing activities (Crenshaw, 2005, 2006b, 2007, 2008) to approach more safely these powerful life experiences but the choice needs to be the child's and the child's choice should be honored and respected. Only under these conditions will the child experience therapy as a safe and healing context.

Acknowledge the Reality of the Loss

Children can't begin the grieving process until they first accept the reality of the loss. When sudden, unexpected, or overwhelming losses occur the need to deny the reality is strong. In the case of a traumatic death such as a drive-by shooting, the sense of shock, disbelief, and numbing of feeling all serve to block full awareness and the affective impact of the tragic death. Of course such defenses are adaptive in the acute stages of a sudden and untimely death, but should they persist it will block the mourning process from moving ahead. In the case of major disasters such as airplane crashes, military casualties, natural disasters, or terrorist acts, the grieving process may be inhibited until the body is recovered because the loss may not be real to the survivor. For children who have faced multiple devastating losses, the trauma of such events may necessitate the numbing of their response to subsequent losses that may take the form of lack of acknowledgment, particularly on an affective level.

Recover and Preserve Positive Memories

Cohen and Mannarino (2004; see also Cohen, Mannarino, & Deblinger, 2006) included the task of preserving positive memories in their traumatic grief model. But before they can be preserved they have to be recovered, a task that may be especially difficult in the case of traumatic grief because trauma dysregulates and disrupts memory systems (Schore, 2003a, 2003b; Siegel, 1999; Siegel & Hartzell, 2003). It is critical to youth who either have few positive memories or when their access is blocked due to exceedingly painful or traumatic circumstances of the death, to recover these happy memories. When youth have lost so much, these positive memories become all the more priceless.

Especially helpful are memories related to "stories of attachment" (Crenshaw, 2002). Photographs of being held and cherished by a deceased parent, grandparent, or older sibling helps to concretize in the mind of children that they were once loved and wanted by those no longer present to affirm it. Stories told to others by the deceased loved one emphasizing the love they felt for the child are enormously helpful. The recovery and preservation of positive memories plays a key role in creating a coherent narrative memory. We frequently encourage the child and family to bring photographs of happy occasions to the session and highlight these special moments in an effort to solidify these memories. Likewise, in family sessions we solicit "stories of attachment" as well as past statements of the deceased family member expressing love for the children.

By providing associations with the sensory comforts of early caregiver experiences, artifacts and anecdotes of the deceased also serve as hidden regulators, helping to bring the frontal cortex back "online" in the wake of separation and loss. These hidden regulators mediate the long-term effects of early losses by supporting the formation of mental representations that organize the child's affective experiences (Hofer, 1994a, 1994b).

Honor the Timeless Attachments

In the grieving process, often the emphasis and focus is on what is lost which is understandable since loss can be devastating, but focus and emphasis also needs to be placed on what child grievers can hold on to (Klass, Silverman & Nickman, 1996; Shimshon, 1999; Silverman, 1999; Walter, 1996). They can hold on to the attachment to their loved one because that attachment is timeless. The lessons taught, the values internalized, the positive identifications with their loved one, the influence of the person no longer here endures. In a sense we carry in our heart always the influence, the spirit, the teachings, and the love of the special person who is no longer here physically.

As clinicians and counselors it becomes vitally important as to where we put the punctuation. Do we focus disproportionately on what has been lost or do we sensitively balance the sense of loss with an emphasis on the enrichment and gains of our having had such a special person in our lives, if even for a short time? This consideration is all the more cogent when working with youth whose losses are beyond words. While the child griever must let go of the physical person, there is a timeless attachment to their loved one that survives death and this knowledge can bring great comfort and solace.

Children rely on their attachment with their deceased parent to complete their development and "consult" with their deceased parent at critical junctures. They can easily imagine what their parent would advise, unless they were too young to have memories of the parent. In that case it is important for the surviving parent to provide the child with stories and information about the deceased parent that can be incorporated into their identity at each stage of development.

Find Meaning and Create a Coherent Narrative

It is hard to find meaning and perspective when a child's world is turned upside down by repeated or sudden losses of important loved ones. If it is possible to find some positive meaning in an otherwise horrific sense of loss, it will serve the mourner well (Davis, Wortman, Lehman, & Silver, 2000; Neimeyer, 2000).

Neurobiological and attachment research has shown that when children are helped to develop coherent narratives, to make sense and gain perspective when unexpected and horrible things happen to them they are less at risk for traumatic reactions (Cicchetti and Rogosch, 1997; Crenshaw, 2006a; Fonagy and Target, 1997; Harter, 1988; Siegel, 1999; Siegel & Hartzell, 2003). Often, but not always, tragedy brings family members and friends closer together. This may be the only positive consequence that a child can relate to, although older children and teens can sometimes articulate that a devastating loss can re-order their priorities in life and give them a new appreciation of the gift of life.

No one is ever the same after the death of those important to them, but with skillful and compassionate intervention even the traumatically bereaved child can resume gradually a full participation in life with a fresh appreciation of how fragile life is, how precious is the limited, conscious life we are given, and how meaningful are the connections we enjoy with others that makes life even at its worst moments endurable.

REFERENCES

Bellamy, C. (2005). *The state of the world's children 2005: Childhood under threat.* New York: United Nations' Children's Fund.

Cicchetti, D., & Rogosch, R. A. (1997). Self organization [Special issue]. *Development and Psychopathology, 9* (4), 797–815.

Cohen, J., Goodman, R., Brown, E., & Mannarino, A. (2004). Treatment of childhood traumatic grief: Contributing to a newly emerging condition in the wake of community trauma. *Harvard Review of Psychiatry, 12,* 213–16.

Cohen, J., & Mannarino, A. (2004). Treatment of childhood traumatic grief. *Journal of Clinical Child and Adolescent Psychology, 33,* 819–31.

Cohen, J, Mannarino, A., & Deblinger, E. (2006). *Treating trauma and traumatic grief in children and adolescents.* New York: Guilford Press.

Cohen, J., Mannarino, A., & Knudsen, K. (2004). Treating Childhood Traumatic Grief: A pilot study. *Journal of the American Academy of Child & Adolescent Psychiatry, 43,* 1225–33.

Cohen, J., Mannarino, A., & Staron, V. (2006). A pilot study of modified cognitive-behavioral therapy for Childhood Traumatic Grief (CBT-CTG). *Journal of the American Academy of Child & Adolescent Psychiatry, 45,* 1465–73.

Cook, J. M., Schnurr, Paula P., & Foa, E. B. (2004). Bridging the gap between Post-traumatic Stress Disorder research and clinical practice: The example of Exposure Therapy. *Psychotherapy: Theory, Research, Practice, Training, 41,* 374–87.

Crenshaw, D. A. (2002). Disenfranchised grief of children. In Doka, K. (Ed.), *Disenfranchised grief: New directions, challenges, and strategies for practice* (pp. 293–306). Champaign, IL: Research Press.

Crenshaw, D. A. (2005). New clinical tools to address childhood traumatic grief. *Omega: The Journal of Death Studies, 51,* 239–55.

Crenshaw, D.A. (2006a). Neuroscience and trauma treatment: Implications for creative art therapists. In L.C. Carey (Ed.), *Expressive and creative arts methods for trauma survivors* (pp. 21–38). London: Jessica Kingsley Publishers.

Crenshaw, D. A. (2006b). *Evocative strategies in child and adolescent psychotherapy.* Lanham, MD: Jason Aronson.

Crenshaw, D. A. (2007). An interpersonal neurobiological-informed treatment model for childhood traumatic grief. *Omega, 54,* 315–32.

Crenshaw, D. A. (2008). *Therapeutic engagement of children and adolescents: Play, symbol, drawing, and storytelling strategies.* Lanham, MD: Jason Aronson.

Crenshaw, D.A., & Hardy, K.V. (2005). Understanding and treating the aggression of traumatized children in out-of-home care. In N. Boyd-Webb (Ed.), *Working with traumatized youth in child welfare* (pp. 171–95). New York: Guilford Press.

Davis, C. G., Wortman, C. B., Lehman, D. R., & Silver, R. C. (2000). Searching for meaning in loss: Are clinical assumptions correct? *Death Studies, 24,* 497–540.

Didion, J. (2005). *The year of magical thinking.* New York: Knopf.

Doka, K. J. (Ed.). (1989). *Disenfranchised grief: Recognizing hidden sorrow.* Lexington, MA: Lexington Books.

Doka, K. (Ed.). (2002). Disenfranchised grief: *New directions, challenges, and strategies for practice.* Champaign, IL: Research Press.

Foa, E. B., Cahill, S. P., & Pontoski, K. (2004). Factors that enhance treatment outcome of cognitive-behavioral therapy for anxiety disorders. *CNS Spectrums, 9,* 6–17.

Fonagy, P., & Target, M. (1997). Attachment and reflective function: Their role in self-organization. *Development and Psychopathology, 9,* 677–99.

Goodheart, C. D., Kazdin, A. E., & Sternberg, R. J. (Eds.). (2006). *Evidence-based psychotherapy: Where practice and research meet.* Washington, DC: American Psychological Association.

Hardy, K. V., & Laszloffy, T. (2005). *Teens who hurt: Clinical interventions to break the cycle of adolescent violence.* New York: Guilford Press.

Harter, S. (1988). Developmental processes in the construction of the self. In T. D. Yawkey & J. E. Johnson (Eds.), *Integrative processes and socialization: Early to middle childhood* (pp. 45–78). Hillsdale, NJ: Erlbaum.

Hofer, M.A. (1994a). Hidden regulators in attachment, separation, and loss. *Monographs of the Society for Research in Child Development, 59(2–3),* 192–207.

Hofer, M.A. (1994b). Early relationships as regulators of infant physiology and behavior. *Acta Paediatrica. Supplement, 397,* 9–18.

Kandel, E. R. (2005). *Psychiatry, psychoanalysis, and the new biology of mind.* Washington, DC: American Psychiatric Publishing.

Kazdin, A. E. (2005a). Evidence-based assessment for children and adolescents: Issues in measurement development and clinical application. *Journal of Clinical Child and Adolescent Psychology, 34,* 548–58.

Kazdin, A. E. (2005b). Treatment outcomes, common factors, and continued neglect of mechanisms of change. *Clinical Psychology: Science and Practice, 12,* 184–88.

Klass, D., Silverman, P.R., and Nickerman, S. L. (1996). *Continuing bonds: New understandings of grief.* New York: Taylor and Francis Group.

Lieberman, A. F., Compton, N. C., Van Horn, P., & Ippen, C. G. (2003). *Losing a parent to death in the early years: Guidelines for the treatment of traumatic bereavement in infancy and early childhood.* Washington, DC: Zero to Three Publishing/ National Center for Infants, Toddlers, and Families.

Long, G. (2001). *Juniper Tree Burning.* New York: Simon & Schuster.

Long, G. (2007). Fiction. *University of Toronto Quarterly, 76,* 185–96.

Neimeyer, R. A. (2000). Searching for meaning of meaning: Grief therapy and the process of reconstruction. *Death Studies, 24,* 541–58.

Perry, B. D. (1997). Incubated in terror: Neurodevelopmental factors in the "cycle of violence." In J. D. Osofsky (Ed.), *Children in a violent society* (pp. 124–49). New York: Guilford Press.

Perry, B. D. (2005). Applying principles of neurodevelopmental to clinical work with maltreated and traumatized children: The neurosequential model of therapeutics. In N. B. Webb (Ed.), *Working with traumatized youth in child welfare* (pp. 27–52). New York: Guilford Press.

Perry, B. D., & Szalavitz, M. (2006). *The boy who was raised as a dog and other stories from a child psychiatrist's notebook.* New York: Basic Books.

Schore, A. (2003a). *Affect regulation and the repair of the self.* New York: W.W. Norton.

Schore, A. (2003b). *Affect dysregulation and disorders of the self.* New York: W.W. Norton.

Shimshon, S. R. (1999). The Two-Track Model of Bereavement: Overview, retrospect, and prospect. *Death Studies, 23,* 681–714.

Siegel, D. J. (1999). *The developing mind: How relationships and the brain interact to shape who we are.* New York: Guilford Press.

Siegel, D. J., and Hartzell, M. (2003). *Parenting from the inside out: How a deeper self understanding can help you raise children who thrive.* New York: Tarcher/Putnam.

Silverman, P. R. (1999). *Never too young to know: Death in children's lives.* New York: Oxford University Press.

Van der Kolk, B. (2003). The neurobiology of childhood trauma and abuse. *Child and Adolescent Psychiatric Clinics of North America, 12,* 293–317.

Varadarajan, T. (2005). How to read the new portraits of grief: Individualism and death in southeast Asia. *Wall Street Journal,* January 7, 2005.

Walter, T. (1996). A new model of grief: Bereavement and biography. *Mortality, 1,* 7–25.

Webb, N. B. (Ed.) (2002). *Helping bereaved children* (2nd ed.) New York: Guilford Press.

Weisz, J. (2004). *Psychotherapy for children and adolescents: Evidence-based treatments and case examples.* New York: Cambridge University Press.

Weisz, J., & Addis, M. E. (2006). The research-practice tango and other choreographic challenges: Using and testing evidence-based psychotherapies in clinical care settings. In C. D. Goodheart, A. E. Kazdin, & R. J. Sternberg (Eds.), *Evidence-based psychotherapy: Where practice and research meet* (pp. 179–206). Washington, DC: American Psychological Association.

White, M., & Epston, D. (1990). *Narrative means to therapeutic ends.* New York: Norton.

8

A Spectrum of Dynamic Forces That Silence Children

David A. Crenshaw and Jennifer Lee

OVERVIEW

Children speak volumes through their silence. Children can be silent for many reasons. Hardy (2005) explained the sharp distinction between children choosing to remain quiet versus being silenced. Some young children remain quiet because they are timid and shy or anxious which in extreme cases can lead to selective mutism. These children can be helped to find their voice with gentle encouragement and by creating a relaxed natural context for them to speak. Some children may speak loudly but feel silenced because no one is listening anymore. Angry children believe they have to be louder and louder because they don't feel they are being heard. With these children, creating a safe place and time within the family for them to speak and more importantly to be heard can dramatically decrease their anger and acting-out behavior. Other children are silenced because it is not safe for them to speak. Silencing of victims is a core dynamic of oppression of all forms. Sheer terror can literally shut down the neurobiological mechanisms in the brain that underpin speech. Children of terror may not be able to express such events orally. They can, however, be helped to find a different "voice." Finally, children can be silenced by the shame and stigma of their traumatization that renders them voiceless. This chapter explores these forms of silencing of children and ways to help them find their voice.

ANXIETY-BASED SILENCING—SELECTIVE MUTISM

Background

Selective mutism is a childhood disorder of interpersonal communication where a child fails to speak in specific situations where speaking is expected. Such children often refuse to speak in school or to other adults residing outside of the home. The disorder was first identified in 1887 by the German physician Adolf Kussmaul who treated children with *aphasia voluntaria* who refused to speak voluntarily despite having normal speech and language (Krysanski, 2003). In 1934, the Swiss child psychiatrist Moritz Tramer subsequently coined the term *elective mutism* and believed that children with the condition elected not to speak in certain situations (Krysanski, 2003; Standart & Le Couteur, 2003). This term was retained in the 3rd edition of the *Diagnostic and Statistical Manual of Mental Disorders* (DSM-III). Later, elective mutism was hypothesized to be a variant of social phobia (Black & Uhde, 1992). The most recent diagnostic classification (DSM-IV-TR) employs the term *selective mutism* to emphasize the selective dependence on social context, and reflects more contemporary beliefs that the disorder is not predominantly a function of oppositional behaviors.

The onset of selective mutism is typically before the age of five, but it is usually detected when the child first attends school. Researchers have noted that transient mutism may be a common condition during transitional periods (Wilkins, 1985); as a result, selective mutism should not be diagnosed within the first month of school. The clinical diagnosis is warranted when the child demonstrates a consistent failure to speak in certain settings, which significantly interferes with normal psychosocial functioning.

The prevalence rates of this disorder are very low and found in less than 1% of children seen in mental health centers (APA, 2000). This rare disorder is oftentimes frustrating and perplexing to parents of affected children, given the evidence and capacity of normal language production at home. In situations that render a child mute, communication can sometimes be expressed through gestures, shaking or nodding the head, and in some cases, monosyllabic utterances (APA, 2000).

The etiology of Selective Mutism has been debated since its conception. Although several factors have been described—including exposure to childhood trauma, developmental disorders, oppositional behaviors, and temperament qualities like extreme shyness—there is little consensus on the underlying factors that contribute to the manifestation of the disorder. Cohan, Price, and Stein (2006) proposed a developmental psychopathology perspective of Selective Mutism, integrating biological, temperamental, psychological, developmental, and social/environmental processes. In their review of the literature, the authors found that anxiety is a characteristic feature of the majority of selectively mute children, and appears to be an important vulnerability factor in the development of the disorder. A hypothetical pathway may start with a child who experiences heightened levels of anxiety, as a result of a strong genetic loading for anxiety or a behaviorally inhibited temperament. The child may exhibit increased sensitivity to verbal interactions with others, triggered by an environmental stressor such as interpersonal trauma, change of schools, or death of a loved one. The resulting condition is the child's failure to speak in a specific setting despite having the ability to do so in other settings.

The anxiety associated with selective mutism is but one form of silencing that affects children. The overwhelming anxiety these children experience in certain settings can be countervailed by the creation of a safe therapeutic milieu, as illustrated in the following case presentation. The case described was treated with play therapy methods. A review of all the different treatment options for selective mutism is beyond the scope of this chapter.

A Clinical Example: Melissa[1]

I[2] owe a huge debt of gratitude to Melissa, a six-year-old girl, who taught me a lot about how to approach and how not to work with selective mutism. Melissa was a strong-willed first grader, the youngest of four children, with three older brothers. She had frustrated the efforts of a large number of dedicated school personnel who had done their best to encourage her to talk in school to no avail. She had gone to nursery school, and kindergarten, and was now in the fifth month of her first grade year without uttering a single word in school. At home she was quite talkative within her immediate family but often did not speak in the presence of grandparents, aunts, uncles, and cousins much to the consternation of her parents and the extended family.

The family entertained high hopes at the beginning of the school year because the first grade teacher was a friend of the family and is an extremely capable and experienced teacher and both the teacher and the parents were quite optimistic that Mrs. Roberts would be able to get Melissa to talk in school. When that did not happen and the school year entered the second half a great sense of urgency arose in the family and Mrs. Roberts was feeling increasing pressure. The school psychologist and social worker had been called in earlier in the year to render their assistance and the school social worker had seen Melissa on a weekly basis at school but even in the one-to-one situation of the school counseling, Melissa would play but not speak. The school social worker who had been for several years in a supervision group I conduct for therapists, said to the family and teacher, "If anyone can get Melissa to speak, Dr. Crenshaw can." What a set-up.

The parents' expectations were high and after eight sessions they were greatly disappointed and concerned that in spite of my best efforts and attempts Melissa was not speaking in the sessions. I had treated other children with Selective Mutism using a variety of approaches, usually a combination of individual play therapy and family therapy and never before found it so difficult to facilitate the child's "coming to voice." At that point, I engaged in some serious "soul searching." It paid off handsomely.

I realized that as a result of the build-up by my supervisee, "I had something to prove." I understood that whenever this attitude infiltrates our therapeutic work, it becomes an obstacle to success. Prior to my next visit with Melissa, in spite of the growing impatience of her parents, I decided that I would adjust my mindset and dispense with all expectations that she would speak, rather I would just focus on being fully in the moment with her and see what, if anything happens.

During the course of play we engaged in hide and seek play, as we had done in some prior sessions using the puppets to hide and to also seek. She hid a bear puppet and I built up as much suspense as I could as I used the frog puppet to look for the bear. When I spotted the hidden puppet, I loudly exclaimed, "I found the elephant!" She shouted, "You did not, you found the bear!" She looked like she was in shock but I tried not to punctuate the moment, rather I simply replied matter-of-factly, "My mistake. It's my turn to pick a puppet to hide and you are not going to be able to find the parrot!" She said, "Yes, I will." In the next few sessions, she retreated somewhat in that she would whisper in the ears of the puppets what she wanted to say but it was audible enough for me to hear it so I just replied as if she were speaking in a normal voice. After ten sessions she talked nearly non-stop and she was loud and boisterous like she had always been at home.

It is interesting that when the family reported this breakthrough to her teacher, the teacher expressed some chagrin to my supervisee that basically that "hot-shot" psychologist in Rhinebeck got her to talk but "Big deal, she is still not talking in school, so what good is it." Mrs. Roberts was right. Unless Melissa was able to talk at school the therapy had accomplished very little. So the next time I saw Melissa with her family, I announced that we are going to have a contest. She was very interested in this idea. I told her that whoever won the contest would be awarded a prize that I negotiated with her family. Her parents, Melissa, her three brothers and I were the participants in the contest. We each would make a guess as to what day— Monday, Tuesday, Wednesday, Thursday, or Friday—it would be when Melissa first speaks to Mrs. Roberts. We would also have to guess whether it would be in the morning or afternoon and whether it would be a sunny day or a cloudy day. So we all wrote down our choices. Melissa's oldest brother helped her to write out her choices and then we put all the guesses in a jar. The next week, Melissa raced excitedly into the office and shouted that she had won. She said, "It was Tuesday, in the morning, and it was a sunny day." Melissa claimed her prize of being taken out for pizza as the guest of honor in the family. Mrs. Roberts was very happy although I later heard that Melissa had become a bit of a chatterbox and was somewhat disruptive at times in class.

The psychodynamics of children like Melissa with selective mutism can be complex but a common pattern that I have observed is that often these children are somewhat anxious or fearful by temperament. Often they have older siblings who talk for them when they are timid and shy. Adults at some point begin to pressure the kids when they refuse to talk. This serves to increase anxiety about vocalization and has the secondary complication of placing the children in a position of considerable power. Although anxious, many of these children are strong-willed like Melissa. I initially fell into the trap by joining with all the other adults who had a need for Melissa to talk, in my case to demonstrate that I could live up to the lofty expectations of the referral source and the family. Inadvertently, the same dynamics that had maintained her silence were duplicated in the therapist's office. It was only after I realized the mistake that I was making and adjusted my expectations that Melissa was able to come to voice in our sessions. Using the same playful approach it became a natural extension of our work to extend these gains to her functioning in school. Play therapy is a natural choice for problems of selective mutism because play has inherent healing qualities; it is disarming, and it reduces anxiety, naturally desensitizing children to their fears.

I will be forever grateful to Melissa. I learned a lot from my work with her. Since then I always keep in mind the lessons she taught me when working with children with selective mutism. It has not taken more than eight sessions with any of the ten children I have seen subsequently to overcome their self-imposed silence. Four of the children spoke during the first session. Please note short-term therapy would not be expected to be effective if trauma has contributed to the selective mutism. Also there may be secondary effects of the selective mutism such as depression, low self-esteem, or social problems that may need to be addressed as well. Enabling the child to speak is an important first step but usually not the last step in the therapy process.

When a new child with selective mutism comes to my office for the first time, I make sure that there is no demand placed on them to speak. In fact, when I greet them, I don't really give them the opportunity to speak and thereby passing over that moment when they typically "freeze." I typically just say, "Hello Suzie, come in, let me show you and your parents my office. I want you to see some of the toys and play things that we can use together." I have learned not to place any premium on the child's communication to me, which just increases his/her anxiety and reduces the chance of success. They break their silence when it is natural for them to do so in the context of a playful and relaxed therapeutic context that play therapy uniquely provides. I never cease to be amazed what children can teach us.

FEAR-BASED SILENCING—OPPRESSION

Silencing of victims is a core dynamic of oppression of all forms. Children who are exposed to violence, abuse, discrimination, threats, explicit or veiled, will not speak because it is dangerous to do so. Children may also lose their voice because of discrimination and oppression related to gender inequality, sexual orientation, growing racial/ethnic differences, and economic disparity.

Beginning with the writings of Carol Gilligan (1982; 1990) there has been recognition that in Western culture males are socialized to hinge their self-worth on instrumental accomplishments, in contrast to girls whose self-worth is closely tied to their self-perception of their ability to form and maintain caring relationships (Frank & Thomas, 2003). Four patterns that contribute to the "self-silencing" of girls were identified by Jack and Dill (1992). Elaborating on the work of Gilligan they noted that when girls judge themselves, they are highly influenced by peer evaluations or what they call "externalized self-perceptions." Girls are also likely to "silence" their thoughts, needs, feelings, and opinions to avoid confrontations and conflict with others. Another contributing factor is the tendency of girls to solidify their relationships with others by the pattern of putting themselves in a secondary role, by placing a higher priority on the needs of others than their own. Finally, they tend to minimize their anger and hostility in order to comply with the culturally imposed expectations that they present themselves as caring, nurturing, and compliant (Frank & Thomas, 2003).

Gay, lesbian, and transgender youth are often silenced in damaging ways by the dominant culture. Both overt and covert forms of homophobia is pervasive in schools, churches and other community places, not to mention families and exerts a powerful silencing force that has a profound deleterious psychological impact on these youth (Baker, 2002). Garbarino and de-Lara (2002) documented the devastating impact of the taunting, bullying, and harassment that gay and lesbian youth suffer daily from homophobic peers. They point out that homophobia is so prevalent that "boys particularly live in fear that any act of same-sex kindness or affection is going to be interpreted as a homosexual gesture and thus invoke homophobic sexual harassment" (p. 91). Baker (2002), however, stressed the responsibility of adults in creating and perpetuating a "culture of silence" about homophobia by failing to protect gay children and by promoting the belief that homosexuality is shameful, immoral, and unnatural.

Gay, lesbian, and bisexual youth are at greater risk for suicidal ideation and attempts than their heterosexual peers. A study at the University of Minnesota revealed that in a survey of nearly 22, 000 sexually active ninth- and twelfth-grade students in Minnesota, there were 2,255 who reported same-gender sexual experience (Eisenberg & Resnick, 2006). The results of the study further revealed that over half of the gay, lesbian, and bi-sexual youth had thought about suicide and a striking number (34%) had made a suicide attempt. The researchers found that the risk factors associated with gay, lesbian, or bi-sexual orientation could be mediated by the protective factors of school connectedness, adult caring, and school safety. Gay, lesbian and bisexual youth, however, reported significantly lower levels of these protective factors than their heterosexual peers.

As vigorously as children attempt to avoid voicing and facing the pain of their woundedness, an equally strong desire emanating from the healthy, core self longs to unburden, to share their story, to have it witnessed and honored by a trusted other. When a child learns to trust a healer, who listens with empathy, the wounded spirit of the child, that has been shrouded in shame and secrecy, and encased in darkness, is able to emerge into the light and warmth of acceptance and genuine caring of one human being for another.

Race and class are potent cultural forces that also foment and intimidate those members who are not considered a part of the dominant culture (Hardy & Laszloffy, 2005; Miller & Stiver, 1997). This force is so pervasive and powerful that the silence about these shaping forces permeates even therapy rooms, which should be at least one place that these sensitive issues can be discussed openly. In a recent training session, I showed a brief clip of a film in which race, class, and culture were defining and shaping forces in the life of the family portrayed. The training group consisted of a number of seasoned clinicians. When I asked the group what they observed in the clip, not one person mentioned race, class, or cultural influences. When I pointed this out they were as shocked as I was that the enveloping and pervasive influence of silencing makes it hard to even talk about these sensitive issues that play a defining role in the lives of many children and families.

Sometimes the larger relational world context which includes culture and the historical moment in time in which we live is so poisonous it can inflict devastating blows to the spirit of children and render them voiceless. Garbarino (1995; 1999) and Hardy (Hardy & Laszloffy, 2005) delineated the devastating role of sociocultural trauma and social toxicity on our youth. Some social conditions are so toxic to the healthy development of our youth that they overwhelm even the best of developmental assets as defined by the Search Institute (Benson & Leffert, 2001) including resilience in youth and favorable social support systems. The Search Institute (http://www.search-institute.org/aboutsearch/) is an independent nonprofit organization whose mission is to provide resources to promote healthy children, youth, and communities. The Institute developed a list of 40 developmental assets that are critical to the healthy growth of youth. The program also identified risk factors that undermine the healthy growth and development of our youth.

Garbarino (1999) in his classic book on the subject of violent male youths, *The Lost Boys*, cited the work of Tolan (1996) who studied youth in the most violent neighborhoods of Chicago and summarized his findings in a paper with the intriguing title of "How Resilient Is the Concept of Resilience?" In the worst cases of high crime neighborhoods, extreme poverty, and highly stressed families, Tolan found no examples of resilient youth as defined in the study by being no more than one year behind grade level in school and not requiring mental health intervention. When youngsters are silenced by the toxicity of their social and cultural context the concept of resilience has little resilience.

Garbarino and Hardy argued that sociocultural trauma is the most neglected and the most insidious of all forms of trauma studied. In the residential treatment of children far too many "voiceless" boys and girls show up for admission with horrifying life stories marked by exposure to violence, the scars of poverty, victims of various forms of devaluation and marginalization by society. As Garbarino and Hardy explained, these youngsters typically suffer from sociocultural trauma including profound and multiple losses that in many cases were not properly recognized or adequately treated. Not surprisingly these youth show up in clinics, day treatment centers, and ultimately residential treatment centers or in some especially tragic cases, youth detention centers, filled with deep sorrow and seething rage.

These boys and now also girls, in greater numbers, are often judged in a narrow and simplistic way as "just bad kids." Those who end up in youth detention centers in most cases will not be recognized as boys and girls suffering from devastating emotional wounds but simply as kids who are placed away from their homes and communities for "correction." What they really need is a healing "connection" with caring, committed, and trustworthy adults. Even when placed in mental health facilities they do not always receive adequate treatment as noted by Greenwald (2002) who observed that youth diagnosed with conduct disorder have histories replete with loss and trauma and yet few of the programs, at that time, offered trauma-informed treatment.

In recent years, the treatment of these youngsters has taken a hopeful and constructive turn. An increasing number of residential treatment programs have adopted the Sanctuary Model for trauma-informed treatment developed by Sandra Bloom (2005) originally for inpatient treatment of adults, but is now being adapted for residential treatment of children (Farragher & Yanosky, 2005). Another encouraging treatment program that addresses the unbearable grief and sorrow of these youngsters is the traumatic grief protocols developed by Cohen, Mannarino, and Deblinger (2006). This evidence-based treatment program for traumatic grief is being widely used with children and represents a significant breakthrough and hopeful advancement in the treatment of our most severely wounded children. (See Chapter 7 for more detailed information on child traumatic grief protocols.)

TERROR-BASED SILENCING—DIRECT THREATS TO REMAIN SILENT

Children speak volumes through their silence. Terror silences far too many children. They don't speak for fear of further torment or they are unable to use language to describe their experience because trauma shuts down the language processing areas of the brain (Van der Kolk, 2002, 2003). Jan Goodwin (2004) described the horrifying experiences of young Congolese girls in her article in *The Nation*. She reported the rape of children as young as two or three years old. She told of a six-year-old girl who was carried kicking and screaming into the bushes by armed militia who gang-raped her. The child nearly starved to death before she was found. She could neither walk nor talk and required surgical repair of the internal damage she suffered, not to mention the psychic trauma this child suffered that rendered her voiceless. Inwardly they may be screaming in anguish but in the face of terror children are rendered voiceless. It is difficult to retain a voice when a child is literally as Perry (1997) observed "incubated in terror." An important goal of trauma-informed therapy is to help children reclaim their voice.

Liem (2007) in a study of Korean-Americans centered on their personal and family experiences of the Korean War concluded that silence about historical trauma is common among survivors. The silence often creates impediments to healing and recovery and serves as a conduit through which the intergenerational effects of catastrophic experiences are transmitted. Liem explained that the silence, in which memories of unresolved trauma reside, is enforced by a combination of state, community, family, and the silencing power of the trauma itself. Thus, the power of trauma to silence its victims can span multiple generations.

The vital necessity of reparative approaches to the woundedness of our youth was ably expressed by Adelman (1995) who stated, "Experiences of trauma lead to changes in the self, which provide the vehicle for intergenerational transmission of trauma" (p. 385). The woundedness impacts subsequent generations, who grow up in the emotional milieu stemming from the injured spirit of the previous generation and shaped by the impact of a trauma they never directly experienced and perhaps was never openly revealed.

Since terrifying experiences can literally render a person via neurobiological mechanisms voiceless, trauma-informed therapies have incorporated into their treatment protocols non-verbal interventions including a wide range of play, art, movement, dance, EDMR, and creative arts methods (Carey, 1998, 2006; Cohen, Mannarino, & Deblinger, 2006; Crenshaw, 2006; Gil, 2006). A good cross-cultural example is a program developed by the Center for the Victims of Torture in Sierra Leone to treat the aftermath of war atrocities relies on the healing power of symbolization (Stepakoff, 2007). The program makes use of both expressive therapy techniques as well as indigenous healing practices including songs, drawings, drama, cultural stories, letter writing, dance, movement, and rituals. Silence is viewed as complicating the psychological harm of the war atrocities, and repair comes through giving voice to their experiences either through non-verbal or verbal expression or the combination of both (Stepakoff, 2007). While giving voice to the unspeakable terror is an essential healing ingredient, it is not required that it be an oral voice. The body may give voice through movement or dance therapies or EMDR, and may be expressed through art, music, or other creative art therapy activities.

It is not unusual for children to be directly threatened bodily harm if they ever tell of the abuse they suffered (Crenshaw, Boswell, Guare, & Ying-Ling, 1986; Crenshaw & Mordock, 2004; Crenshaw, Rudy, Triemer, & Zingaro, 1986). Forced silence has often been a secondary source of trauma layered on the original abuse experiences these children suffered (see the story of Lizzie in Chapter 10). For these children helping them regain their voice requires slow, patient, empathic, and compassionate work to build sufficient trust in the therapeutic relationship that they feel safe enough to disclose the unspeakable in whatever voice they find most accessible. We never cease to be amazed by the courage these children manifest when they break their silence.

SHAME-BASED SILENCING—STIGMA ASSOCIATED WITH TRAUMATIC ABUSE

When terrorized children are rendered mute, they may also be confronted with societal forces that perpetuate and exacerbate their silencing. As with sexual traumatization, the shame and associated stigma may force affected individuals to be without a voice. According to the U.S. Department of Justice, only 36% of rapes and 34% of attempted rapes were reported to police in the period from 1992 to 2000 (Rennison, 2002). This same report indicated that only 26% of sexual assaults toward females were reported to police.

Young women in college reported the following reasons as barriers to breaking their silence when they have been sexually victimized: 1) the incident would be viewed as their fault; 2) they would feel ashamed; 3) they did not want anyone to know about the incident; and 4) they did not want the police to be involved (Thompson, Sitterle, Clay, & Kingree, 2007). Similar pressures silence many young women in the work place who are reluctant to report various forms of sexual harassment. It is sad to recognize that girls and women are silenced in such a wide range of ways and settings in our culture even when their most intimate space, their sexuality, is violated though we pride ourselves on our commitment to human rights. Such violations cause injury to the spirit of the person, yet their voices are silenced— it is heartbreaking, it is outrageous.

Perhaps the most heartbreaking of all experiences along the healing path is when children courageously break their silence, but are not believed. Children are without question suggestible. Therapists should never assume abuse or ask leading questions. The proper stance for the therapist is to keep an open and receptive mind in exploring the child's experience without any preconceived notions. But there are children who carry the deep and secret wound of abuse sometimes for years and finally with fear and trepidation work up the courage to tell someone they trust, perhaps a parent, and are then devastated because they are not believed, and perhaps even worse, are blamed. Such was the case with Linda, whose story is told in Chapter 10.

Younger clinicians and students in our field may be surprised in light of how many books are available today on sexual abuse to know that incest was shrouded in an eerie silence until relatively recently. Freud, under pressure from the Victorian values of the historical moment of time in which he lived, revised his theory of incest as a cause of neuroses in favor of fantasies of incest. Consequently, incest was a rather taboo topic in the field until the publication of Suzanne Sgroi's book, *Handbook of Clinical Intervention in Child Sexual Abuse,* in 1981. Sgroi was invited to speak at a conference in 1983, sponsored by the Astor Home for Children, and she told me at that time, how amazing it was to her that just one publication on the topic had made her a nationally known expert on the issue at that time. Since then, of course, there has been a plethora of writings on this once forbidden subject.

A defining moment in my confrontation with that eerie silence that prevailed for decades after Freud was effectively silenced on the issue of incest, happened when I was 18 years old. I was working at a Mental Hospital in the Midwest as a Ward Attendant while also starting college. During the decade of the 1960s, I worked and received training in several public, large mental hospitals. In comparison to mental health services offered today, that even now are beset by shortcomings, in the early 1960s they were primitive, particularly in the back wards of some publically operated mental hospitals.

I must be careful not to be too self-righteous in my judgment of these institutions of the past. I am sure many good and well-intended people worked hard and did their best to help the patients in their care. A book, *Evolution of a Missouri Asylum: Fulton State Hospital, 1851–2006* (Lael, Brazos, & McMillen, 2007) reminds us that "best practices" are relative to the historical moment in time. Treatments such as water treatments, lobotomies, and straitjackets were once "best practices" although they seem primitive by today's standards. We need not be harsh in our judgments of those methods that now seem so drastic and harsh lest we suffer the same disdain when our current methods are reviewed by those who come later.

It is interesting that Fulton State Hospital (I never worked at Fulton State) was the first such mental hospital founded west of the Mississippi in 1851 (Lael, Brazos, & McMillen, 2007). The story behind its founding is also fascinating. It took a tragic event to prompt the public and politicians to build an "asylum for lunatics" as compared to the prior practice of putting them in jails. The sad event that triggered this reform was the death of the seventh Governor of the State of Missouri, Thomas Reynolds, who in the Governor's mansion tied a piece of twine around the trigger of his rifle and shot himself in February 1844 (Lael, Brazos, & McMillen, 2007).

The large state hospitals up until the 1970s were populated largely by people who were considered too impaired to receive more than custodial care and they were warehoused in large, depressing institutions, some with 30,000 patients or more. Some of the buildings of these mammoth institutions still stand as relics to remind us of the primitive, shameful care by today's standards, these patients and their families were offered.

When I worked the back wards of one of these mental hospitals, I had an experience that has haunted me ever since. The buildings where this patient who I will call Maude (fictitious name) was housed were torn down long ago and the patients long ago removed, but Maude remains with me in a disturbing way that I can never put to rest. Maude was in her 60s at the time but she had been sent to the hospital at age 13. At the time that I was working there it had been 40 years since she had a family visitor. The spirit of the person residing in the frail shell of her human body had died long before I met her. There was no person alive, no spirit, the flame had been extinguished, no one to converse with, no one to make contact with, just an empty shell—a corpse still walking around, eating a little, attending to basic bodily functions and nothing else. She would sit in the day room and stare off into space with utter vacancy. I tried numerous times to see if I could awaken the person who once resided within but she was no longer there.

The story of what brought her to the hospital in the early 1900s fills me with horror, shame, and disgust to this very day. She dared to share a story of incest in a time and era when such stories were not believed and more often led to blame and punishment, if not exile from the family. Such was the case with Maude. Although there is no way to know for certain that she was given a diagnosis for psychosis and admitted to the hospital, simply because she accused her father of incest, the mere possibility is deeply disturbing. Remember it was around 1910 when she made the accusation. In those days, it was not uncommon to think that anyone who would make an accusation of incest must be "crazy."

I don't think I will ever fully recover from the shock of learning what may have been the true but unacknowledged story of Maude's life. Assuming that she was not psychotic at age 13, and the only data offered to support the psychosis was her accusation of incest, she dared to break her silence. What courage that must have taken. She was exiled forever, in a dank, dark, and depressing institution for the rest of her life. Her body was still housed there when I met Maude, but her spirit had left that dehumanizing place long before. You can imprison a body but not the soul.

John O'Donohue (1999) observed that our inner wounds call out for healing. He stated, "There is no one—regardless of how beautiful, sure, competent, or powerful—who is not damaged internally in some way. Each of us carries in our hearts the wound of mortality. We are particularly adept at covering our inner wounds, but no wound is ever silent" (p. 178). Since no wound is ever silent may there always be an empathic healer present and listening so children don't suffer the anguish of bearing their pain alone.

REFERENCES

Adelman, A. (1995). Traumatic memory and the intergenerational transmission of Holocaust narratives. *The Psychoanalytic Study of the Child, 50,* 343–67.

American Psychiatric Association (APA) (2000). *Diagnostic and statistical manual of mental disorders (4th ed., text revision).* Washington, DC: Author.

Baker, J. M. (2002). *How homophobia hurts children: Nurturing diversity at home, at school, and in the community.* New York: Haworth Press.

Benson, P. L., & Leffert, N. (2001). Childhood and adolescence: Developmental assets. In N. J. Smelser & P. G. Baltes (Eds.), *International encyclopedia of the social and behavioral sciences* (pp. 1690–97). Oxford: Pergamon.

Black, B., & Uhde, T. W. (1992). Elective mutism as a variant of social phobia. *Journal of the American Academy of Child and Adolescent Psychiatry, 31,* 1091–94.

Bloom, S. (2005). Creating sanctuary for kids: Helping children heal from violence. *Therapeutic Communities: The International Journal for Therapeutic and Supportive Organizations, 26,* 1–7.

Carey, L. (1998). *Sand play therapy with children and families.* Northvalle, NJ: Jason Aronson.

Carey, L. (Ed.) (2006). *Expressive and creative arts methods for trauma survivors.* London: Jessica Kingsley Publishers.

Cohan, S. L., Price, J. M., & Stein, M. B. (2006). Suffering in silence: Why a developmental psychopathology perspective on selective mutism is needed. *Developmental and Behavioral Pediatrics, 27,* 341–54.

Cohen, J., Mannarino, A. & Deblinger, E. (2006). *Treating trauma and traumatic grief in children and adolescents.* New York: Guilford Press.

Crenshaw, D. A. (2006). *Evocative strategies in child and adolescent psychotherapy.* Lanham, MD: Rowman & Littlefield Publishers.

Crenshaw, D., Boswell, J., Guare, R., & Ying-Ling, C. (1986). Intensive psychotherapy of repeatedly and severely traumatized children. *Residential Group Care and Treatment, 3,* 17–36.

Crenshaw, D. A., & Mordock, J. B. (2004). An ego-strengthening approach with multiply traumatized children: Special reference to the sexually abused. *Residential Treatment of Children and Youth, 23,* 1–18.

Crenshaw, D., Rudy, C., Triemer, D., & Zingaro, D. (1986). Psychotherapy with abused children: Breaking the silent bond. *Residential Group Care and Treatment, 3,* 25–38.

Eisenberg, M. E., & Resnick, M. D. (2006). Suicidality among gay, lesbian and bisexual youth: The role of protective factors. *Journal of Adolescent Health, 39,* 662–68.

Farragher, B., & Yanosky, S. (2005). Creating a trauma-sensitive culture in residential treatment. *Therapeutic Community: The International Journal for Therapeutic and Supportive Organizations, 26,* 97–113.

Frank, J. B., & Thomas, C. D. (2003). Externalized self-perceptions, self-silencing, and the prediction of eating pathology. *Canadian Journal of Behavioural Science, 35,* 219–28.

Garbarino, J. (1995). *Raising children in socially toxic environments.* San Francisco: Jossey-Bass.

Garbarino, J. (1999). *Lost boys: Why our sons turn violent and how we can save them.* New York: Anchor Books, A Division of Random House.

Garbarino, J., & deLara, E. (2002). *And words can hurt forever.* New York: The Free Press.

Gil, E. (2006). *Helping abused and traumatized children: Integrating directive and nondirective approaches.* New York: Guilford Press.

Gilligan, C. (1982). *In a different voice: Psychological theory and women's development.* Cambridge, MA: Harvard University Press.

Gilligan, C. (1990). Teaching Shakespeare's sister: Notes from the underground of female adolescence. In C. Gilligan, N. Lyons, & T. J. Hanmer (Eds.), *Making connections: The relational worlds of adolescent girls at Emma Willard School* (pp. 6–29). Cambridge, MA: Harvard University Press.

Goodwin, J. (2004). Silence=rape. *The Nation.* March 8. Available from: http://www.thenation.com/doc/20040308/goodwin

Greenwald, R. (2002). The role of trauma in conduct disorder. *Journal of Aggression, Maltreatment & Trauma, 6,* 5–23.

Hardy, K. V. (2005). *Working with low-income families.* Presentation at the Ackerman Institute for the Family. New York.

Hardy, K. V., & Laszloffy, T. (2005). *Teens who hurt: Clinical interventions to break the cycle of adolescent violence.* New York: Guilford Press.

Jack, D., & Dill, D. (1992). The Silencing the Self Scale: Schemas of intimacy associated with depression in women. *Psychology of Women Quarterly, 16,* 97–106

Krysanski, V. L. (2003). A brief review of selective mutism literature. *Journal of Psychology, 137,* 29–40.

Lael, R. L., Brazos, B., & McMillen, M. F. (2007). *Evolution of a Missouri asylum: Fulton State Hospital, 1851–2006.* Columbia: University of Missouri Press.

Liem, R. (2007). Silencing historical trauma: The politics and psychology of memory and voice. *Peace and Conflict: Journal of Peace Psychology, 13*, 153–74.

Miller, J. B., & Stiver, I. P. (1997). *The healing connection: How women form relationships in therapy and life.* Boston: Beacon Press.

O'Donohue, J. (1999). *Eternal echoes: Celtic reflections on our yearning to belong.* New York: Perennial/Harper Collins.

Perry, B. (1997). Incubated in Terror: Neurodevelopmental Factors in the "Cycle of Violence." In J. D. Osofsky (Ed.), [*Children in a Violent Society*] (pp. 124–49). New York: Guilford Press.

Rennison, C. M. (2002). *Rape and sexual assault: Reporting to police and medical attention, 1992–2000.* Washington, DC: USGPO. NCJ 194530.

Sgroi, S. (1981). *Handbook of clinical intervention in child sexual abuse.* New York: The Free Press.

Standart, S., & Le Couteur, A. (2003). The quiet child: A literature review of selective mutism. *Child and Adolescent Mental Health, 8*, 154–60.

Stepakoff, S. (2007). The healing power of symbolization in the aftermath of massive war atrocities: Examples from Liberian and Sierra Leonean survivors. *Journal of Humanistic Psychology, 47*, 400–12.

Thompson, M., Sitterle, D., Clay, G., & Kingree, J. (2007). Reasons for not reporting victimizations to the police: Do they vary for physical and sexual incidents? *Journal of American College Health, 55*, 277–82.

Tolan, P. (1996). How resilient is the concept of resilience? *Community Psychologist 4*, 12–15.

Van der Kolk, B. (2002). In terror's grip: Healing the ravages of trauma. *Cerebrum, 4*, 34–50. New York: The Dana Foundation.

Van der Kolk, B. (2003). The neurobiology of childhood trauma and abuse. *Child and Adolescent Psychiatric Clinics of North America, 12*, 293–317.

Wilkins, R. (1985). A comparison of elective mutism and emotional disorders in children. *British Journal of American Psychiatry, 146*, 196–203.

NOTES

1. This example was first used in an article printed in the Play Therapy Magazine (June, 2007) and is reproduced here with the permission of the Association for Play Therapy.

2. The use of the pronoun "I" throughout the text refers to the first author, David A. Crenshaw.

9

Therapist Healing and Use of Self

David A. Crenshaw

OVERVIEW

Would be healers do not receive an exemption from the heartaches or emotional abrasions that beset those we wish to help. Although every person and every life is unique those who attempt to heal others can readily relate to the emotional pain and suffering that few if any escape entirely on their journey through life. There is a sense in which all healers are wounded just as are those we want to help. The question becomes what to do with our woundedness. It would be a huge mistake and potentially risky to those who seek our help to deny or ignore parts of ourselves that are in need of healing. It is axiomatic in the therapy field that we should seek healing for ourselves before undertaking to heal others.[1] It is crucial, however, to recognize that working with ourselves, striving for growth and health, healing our wounds, is not an isolated task undertaken for a relatively brief period of personal therapy but rather a life long journey in which self-monitoring, personal therapy, supervision, consultation with colleagues, and continuing training and education are vital. It is also essential to pursue a balanced and healthy lifestyle.

The invisible injuries of children, the lacerations to their heart may activate the hidden wounds of the therapist if the healer has not attended to his or her own healing. The primary instrument in the healing process is the self of the therapist. Utmost care is required of that most sensitive of all healing instruments or else we do ourselves as well as those we attempt to heal a great disservice. It is not unusual for therapists to suffer "compassion fatigue" due to neglect of self (Figley, 1995). Therapists tend to be drawn to the field of helping others because of their compassion for others and can easily fall into the habit of putting themselves in a secondary role. This is inevitably a recipe for burn-out.

The importance of the therapist undertaking their own personal therapy cannot be overemphasized. The clinical work we do requires great sensitivity, care in judgment—because some of the therapeutic operations we perform are quite delicate. We can't afford to undertake this work with blind spots, unhealed damage, or unresolved trauma. Freud took time at the end of each work day after seeing his patients to examine his feelings and reactions that were activated in his therapeutic work.

IMPORTANT LESSONS IN HUMILITY

Dr. Walter Bonime, at age 85, confided in me, "I have to work with my reactions all the time—things that I thought I resolved a long time ago can come up in a new form." I greatly admired Dr. Bonime for sharing this with me because it taught me that our work with ourselves is never done. He was a master craftsman in our trade. I have never met anyone who could match his exceptional blend of sharp clinical insight, astute analytical skills conveyed in a compassionate manner. Yet, this man so revered in his field, so learned, with over 50 years of analytical experience told me, "I still work with myself every day." What a humbling lesson for us all.

Another person I consider a unique gift to our field, Olga Silverstein, touched me deeply and also taught me a valuable lesson in humility. Silverstein, in some ways reminded me of Dr. Bonime because she was so incisive. Her verbal facility, ability to go right to the heart of the matter, her wisdom and understanding of families put her in a class of her own in my view. One experience above all, however, was life changing for me. Silverstein in 1987 was the featured presenter for a two-day conference at the Roosevelt Hotel in New York City sponsored by the Ackerman Institute. The Ackerman Institute was founded by Nathan Ackerman, M.D., one of the early pioneers in family therapy.

The conference was a celebration of Olga Silverstein's work with families and what a moving and impressive demonstration of skill, clinical wisdom, and vast experience it turned out to be. At the end of the second day, members of the audience spontaneously stood up and praised her work. In the midst of this shower of superlatives and enthusiastic praise, an amazing thing happened, and I will never forget it. Silverstein became annoyed and somewhat indignant. She made it clear to the audience that she had worked hard over the years to refine her skills and yes, she had a well-developed verbal facility, but she said in effect, "I don't need this. I still have my share of heart-breaking failures."

I can't fully explain how much this meant to me and I have shared this story with every intern and clinician I have supervised since. Recently, I wrote Olga Silverstein and expressed this in person on the occasion of Ackerman Institute's celebration of the work of Olga Silverstein and Peggy Papp, an event held at Hunter College in May of 2007. I also dedicated a recent book to Olga (Crenshaw, 2008). If someone so polished in skill, vastly experienced, so clinically astute and wise as Olga Silverstein said basically, "Wait a minute—don't put me up on a pedestal. I don't want this—because I still have my heart-breaking failures"—she said, in effect, "In spite of all my experience, skills, and wisdom, and all the heart that I put in to my work I still reserve the right to fail—because sometimes we will—as heartbreaking as that may be."

To me this was one of the most liberating experiences of my professional life. Up to that point, I was operating under the illusion that if I studied long enough with the Dr. Bonime's of the world, went to as many of the workshops of the Olga Silverstein's and Salvador Minuchin's of the world as possible, read the books by top practitioners in the field—I would eventually know enough that I would not have to go through any more heart-breaking failures. When I heard Olga Silverstein's words that day I realized that we work in a field where that is an impossible demand.

I still want to learn all I can from the great teachers and masters in the field and read the important books but I realize that doing so and putting all of my heart into the work does not insulate me from the heart-rending experiences of sometimes failing to heal the demolished spirit of a child or a family. This learning was further reinforced by Dr. Bonime when I told him of my experience at Olga Silverstein's presentation. He smiled and said, "I don't like to be put up on a pedestal either. There is not much room to move around up there and it is a long way to fall."

Final Conversations with Walter Bonime

Dr. Bonime was a tremendous inspiration to me. I remember going to New York City on an early morning train, booking a double session with him, sometimes consulting with him about a challenging case, other times talking about theoretical or therapeutic approaches, and most of all his sharing with me his vast experience of nearly half a century of practice, teaching, and writing in psychoanalysis. It was a rare and treasured privilege to learn from such an exceptionally wise and compassionate analyst. Dr. Bonime and Olga Silverstein shared that uncanny ability to go right to the heart of the matter and untangle quickly and incisively a complicated web of emotions, relationships, cultural, and personality factors that sometimes left my head spinning. Dr. Bonime was the model of a clinician I would always aspire to be although, like Olga Silverstein, he was in my mind, in a class of his own. He loved what he did and well into his 80s he would say to me, "David, I am looking forward to not retiring." He also had a wonderful sense of humor. He told me one day, "At my age, I have learned not to say there are two points I want to make—because by the time I make the first one, I can't remember what the other one was."

Dr. Bonime was wonderfully supportive of my work and when he finally did retire I spoke to him on several occasions by phone. One was a very sad call when he told me that his dear wife, Florence, had died. He told me that he had read my book on *Bereavement* several times and found it quite helpful. I just couldn't even imagine that anything I had written could have been helpful to a man who had taught me so much. In these phone calls, Dr. Bonime would say to me, "I want you to call me Walter. We are colleagues now—I want you to call me Walter." That was very difficult for me due to the utmost respect I had for him and the habit of more than 10 years of consultation/study with him during which I always called him, "Dr. Bonime." In our last phone call, I finally managed it and ended the conversation, "Good-bye Walter." Dr. Bonime died at the age of 92. He continued his prolific psychoanalytic writings to the very end.

IN SEARCH OF MY BROTHER'S KEEPER

I've searched high and low,
All around this world,
And nowhere to be found is my brother's keeper,
Surely, he or she must be somewhere,
Belatedly, I came to realize that
My brother's keeper is only to be found,
Within you and me.

—David Crenshaw

I owe a great debt to my late brother Robert. The story of his courage and how he inspired me was originally printed in the *Psychotherapy Networker* (Crenshaw, 2006) in an article called, "In His Footsteps." The expanded story is reprinted below with the kind permission of the Managing Editor, Brett Topping, of the *Psychotherapy Networker*.

My brother Bob was three years older than I, but for as long as I can remember, he always seemed younger, and never more so than on the winter night when he awakened me in our shared bedroom. "David! David! Wake up!" he said in an excited and frightened voice as he leaned over my bed. "I killed somebody, and the body is on the front porch!" I was 11. Outside our bedroom window, snow was falling quietly, as it had for hours. What Bob

Two brothers, Bob, 5 years old and David 2 years old

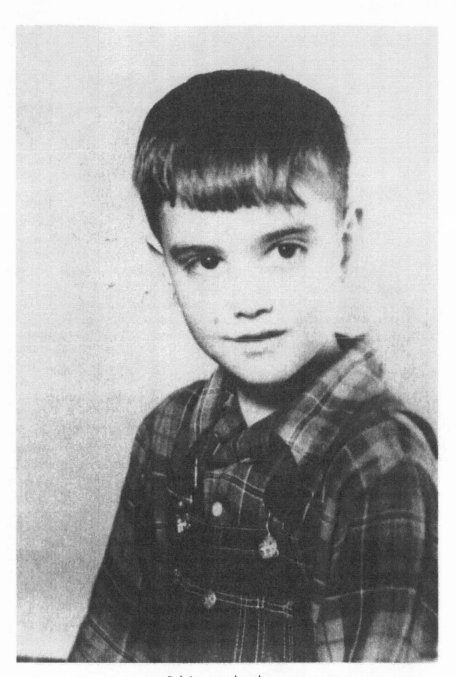

Bob in second grade

was saying to me made no sense, but he was so agitated that, for a moment, I thought in horror that it must be true. As we walked together to the front door, my heart was pounding and my fear so extreme that I could hardly put one foot in front of the other. I flipped the switch to the overhead light and scanned the snow-covered porch. No body. My brother introduced me in that terrifying moment to hallucinations.

A year later, on Christmas morning in 1955, I again woke up in the predawn hours, in the middle of another snowstorm. My brother, now 15, wasn't in his bed. I woke up my parents and together we went out to the front porch. There were tracks leading off it into the snowy darkness.

After throwing on some clothes, my father jumped into the car, while I sat on the hood in my mittens and heavy coat, pointing out Bob's footprints through the heavily blowing snow. We followed his tracks all the way up to Route 169, the main highway running between St. Joseph and Kansas City, Missouri. It was 3 a.m. Visibility was nearly zero, but there were no other cars on the road, so we were easily able to follow the trail Bob had left right down the middle of the highway.

We crawled along for another five miles until, at the bottom of a steep hill locally known as "Happy Hollow," we saw his footprints leave the road, leading behind a collection of large grain silos. There, huddled in his pajamas, with his feet bare, was my frightened and nearly frozen brother. He offered no explanation. He suffered frostbite on his feet, but otherwise survived physically. How anyone could have walked barefoot in deep blowing snow for more than five miles, I still can't understand to this day.

I didn't know exactly then what was wrong with Bob—nobody did—but we sensed that something wasn't quite right. He'd been a "blue baby," suffering anoxia during birth. While I did reasonably well in school and got along well with my friends, he struggled. Now the pressures and stresses of adolescence were driving him toward his first full-blown psychotic episode.

I still remember how hard I tried, over the next few weeks, to reason Bob out of his delusions; how badly I wanted to help him. But all of my gently reasoned talk had no impact whatsoever. I remember that he just sat on his bed in our shared room, staring past me. Among other things, he thought we were poisoning him and refused to eat. He lost a great deal of weight and finally went into a catatonic stupor. My family had no choice but to take him to the state hospital.

On that trip—the first of many over the next three decades—I rode in the backseat with Bob. My dad, who was driving, cried all the way there and all the way home. It was the only time in my life I ever saw my grandfather cry, too—a hard, sobbing cry, just like my father's. My mother only cried a little, but I knew her heart was breaking as well. Families too often feel blamed in these situations, when they feel already an overwhelming burden of guilt.

Bob in sixth grade in band uniform

My parents went out for the evening with some friends; my younger sister was visiting a friend, so I was alone with Bob. He had returned just two months ago from his latest trip to the state hospital after another dramatic decompensation into a catatonic state. He was stabilized at the time, no longer hallucinating or delusional. Bob was 17, and I was 14. Bob confided in me that he wanted to ask a particular girl in his class to go to the prom. In my naïve assessment of the situation, I decided that Bob needed my coaching.

One of the factors that I was certain would work against him was the peculiar way he held his arms. He tended to keep his arms in an elevated position, extended horizontally from the elbows instead of letting them hang relaxed to his sides. This rather bizarre posture invited teasing and ridicule from his peers. I worked all evening coaching him on the "proper way to carry his arms" and helping him with his body posture. We also practiced asking the girl to the prom.

The next day when I saw Bob after school he didn't say much but he didn't have to because it was clear from his pained expression that he had been turned down. Later I found out that the sensitive young lady had declined in the kindest way possible. We never tried that again. I felt that I set him up for another rejection and failure. The following day Bob resumed carrying his arms in the elevated peculiar position that invited further derision from his schoolmates.

From age 15 on, Bob was prone to psychiatric breakdowns that would periodically land him back at the State Hospital. When I was 18, I took a summer job as a ward attendant at the same hospital. Bob was not a patient there at the time. But one night I was working on one of the wards and I was called to go to another ward one floor below to help break up a fight that had broken out between several patients.

When I arrived on the wild scene and assisted the other ward attendants in breaking up the fight, I glanced around the room and there was Bob standing only ten feet away. He had been admitted on an emergency basis that afternoon. My parents did not have a chance to contact me with the disturbing news.

Most of Bob's adolescence was spent battling his combination of neurological and psychiatric impairment as well as trying to finish high school, which he eventually did, although it took him longer because he was on a reduced schedule during the last two years. During most of this period I did not know how to enter my brother's world or even how to communicate with him. He engaged in obsessive writing, pounding out page after page on the old Smith Corona that my Dad bought for him at a garage sale. I still have some of his writings; some were complete scripts for plays. One of his plays featured an actor named Bob Crenshaw. In the play, Bob Crenshaw

Bob, at age 13, before his first psychotic episode

died in January 1990. The play was written by Bob in 1978. He died on January 10, 1990—just one more thing that can't be explained or understood about my brother.

He also wrote volumes about the British Royal Family and much of the writing was total gibberish and made no sense at all. It seemed like once he entered the world of psychosis he was cut off from the rest of us, frequently obsessed with his thoughts and writing, often talking to himself in an animated fashion. But he sometimes would utter words at unexpected times that would stop me in my tracks and break my heart. He would, for example, be pecking away at an intense clip on the Smith Corona and I would say "Good-bye, Bob" on my way out the door to go on a date or to football practice. It would appear that he didn't even hear me. But before I was out the door, he would say, "David, have a good time."

It would have been easier to hear "David, damn you, how come you get to do all the things that I never get to do?" or "What makes you think you deserve a normal life when I've never had one?" Instead, with no malice, no apparent jealousy, sarcasm, or resentment, he left the refuge of his psychotic fog to notice that I was going out and he simply said, "David, have a good time."

Those words pierced my heart because I spent most of my high school career trying to establish that I was "normal" and putting as much distance as I could between the stigma, shame, and embarrassment I felt being connected with my grossly psychiatrically disturbed brother. Bob was so strange, so disturbed, it was easy most of the time to view him in a dehumanized way, not a real person with feelings for others or awareness of those around him. That myth came crashing down each time he would simply say, "David, have a good time."

I am rather proud of a time when I went to bat for my brother. It was a school assembly and my brother was pacing in a corner of the gym with his arms elevated in that habitual peculiar position. He was talking to himself and unwittingly making a spectacle of himself. I cringed when I realized his fly was unzipped. A kid in my class sitting on the bleachers behind me started laughing and making disparaging remarks. I turned around grabbed him by his shirt and lifted him up to my eye level and asked him if he wished to repeat what he had said. The startled kid didn't say a word and fortunately I had the presence of mind to release him and allow him to return to his seat. I deplore violence but I find it hard to feel too badly about this one quite public time that I stood up for Bob.

Throughout those decades, as I underwent my own training as a clinical psychologist and began my career as a therapist, I did whatever I could to help. Bob realized that I was mostly ineffectual, but he did bestow on me one special power—on the occasions when he ran away from my parents' house—he made it a matter of principle to insist that I was the only one who could talk him into coming home. It made me feel that I could help him, at least in this one modest way.

When my brother ran away he always headed for a major highway. He said he was headed for either New York or California. Bob never made it to California but he did make it to New York when he came with my parents to visit my family in 1977.

During the last 25 years of Bob's life he lived with my parents on the farm they bought after I left home to attend college. My mom and dad grew up on farms just a mile apart and fell in love not only with each other but also with life on a farm. Returning to the farm especially for my father made the last three decades of his life the happiest. When Bob ran away from the farm he made a habit of throwing his shoes in one of the ponds on the farm that is closest to the house. Mom thought he did it because he believed he could run faster barefoot, while I wondered if he did it in the hopes that it would help him fight his impulse to run but either way there are still to this day at least twenty pairs of shoes at the bottom of that pond.

My first awareness that my brother was disturbed in his thinking occurred when Bob, some neighborhood kids, and I were shooting baskets in our backyard. I was in third grade, Bob was in sixth grade. While shooting hoops, Bob started mumbling something about Russians. I couldn't understand exactly what he was saying but he was quite agitated and I remember feeling shocked and scared. I don't remember if I said anything to my parents at the time. It is hard to admit something is terribly wrong with your brother and even harder if it is your son. My mother told me recently that my paternal grandfather was the first one to notice something was wrong. My grandpa said when Bob was about a year old, "Something is not right with that boy." Mom said that since Bob was their first child they didn't know and didn't pay any attention to my grandpa at the time.

One day in 1990, my brother sat down for lunch with my mother and began to cry—sobbing in an unusual, wholehearted way—that he couldn't explain. That night, he died unexpectedly in his sleep. Did he know that his life was about to end, and that in some ways, in spite of all the love and care offered by my parents, he had never lived? Not long afterward, my parents gave me his high school class ring, the only worldly possession he'd acquired in his 48 years. I treasure it because I know that the courage and determination it took for Bob to finish high school far surpasses anything that I've ever exhibited. All the therapy in the world will never make it seem right to me that I could have been so privileged and he so tormented.

Life can be so ironic. After my parents had searched during Bob's entire life for answers and sought help from every source they could reasonably access with their limited financial resources (in those days health insurance didn't pay for mental health care), they were excited to learn that the University of Missouri had opened a new multidisciplinary diagnostic center within a hour's drive of their home. They made an appointment to take Bob, hoping that this might lead to a new understanding and some new options for helping Bob. My mom went downstairs at 5:00 a.m. to wake him up for the early morning appointment and found him dead.

I keep that ring to remind me of all that Bob taught me. He taught me my first lessons in humility, lessons repeated many times since I got my license and began to sit and listen to families. Remembering that night in 1955 when my father and I inched down the snowy highway, I accept the fact that I couldn't help my brother in the way I'd have liked to—to have talked him out of his delusions and given him even a portion of my own happiness. All my father and I could do that night was follow his tracks through the snow.

In the same way, I'm not able to help every child and family who seeks my assistance now. All I can do is to remember what Bob taught me—not to blame those who seek my help when I can't help them. Bob didn't make much of an impression on the world outside our family. But he was a masterful teacher for me, and the lessons he taught me accompany me into every therapy session.

That Last "Goodbye"

Because Bob died so suddenly, I did not have a chance to say "good-bye." I reflect occasionally on what I might have said if I could have had that one "last conversation" that we tend to long for when someone we love dies suddenly. I think I would have liked to say, "Bob, I was so absorbed in my quest to prove 'normalcy' I never got to know you, and now I will never get the chance to do so. I think I now understand why you ran away from home so often. I believe you were trying to run away from the inner torment that you have suffered and borne with amazing courage and determination. I could have learned a lot from you if I weren't so scared of something that I couldn't understand or comprehend. As it is, you have taught me more than you will ever know. I can't cross over with you into the world that comes next. We each have to make that crossing alone. I don't know what comes next Bob, nobody does. But I hope the day has finally arrived for you, Bob, to 'have a good time'."

Brothers, Sisters, and Keepers in Today's World

Perhaps the most memorable lesson that Bob taught me is that in the midst of the psychotic fog and haze, the word salad, the scrambled, disorganized thoughts, there resides within a person with a heart, deeply hurting, capable of feeling for others, whose voice needs to be heard. The mental anguish of psychosis can't be appreciated fully by non-sufferers but we can easily imagine the madness that would result from a terrifying night-mare that doesn't end. At the deepest level the message is that these tor-mented minds and hearts are bombarded due to factors that are still today not well understood, more than 65 years after Bob was born, by frighten-ing, bewildering thoughts that leave them cut-off from what makes life endurable—meaningful human relationships.

The insurance companies don't want to pay psychiatrists any more to talk to or more importantly to listen to their patients; they only want to reim-burse psychiatrists for a brief session to figure out what prescription to write. Bob's kindred suffering brothers and sisters today may be on their own in sorting out the bewildering, frightening thoughts that daily torment them. Searching within myself and among my brothers and sisters of our contemporary world I wonder if it would be easier or harder to find today my brother's keeper?

Work with Self on the Invisible Wounds

Whenever a child or a family enters my office with a story about how they have been treated in a shabby or dehumanizing way by the mental health system, the part of me that bears the invisible wounds perks up. I have to work with myself to keep the desire to "rescue" or to rectify the "injustices" of the system. "Rescuing" is neither effective nor a therapeutic operation. I know where the desire comes from because I vividly recall the state hospi-tal (at the time there were no feasible alternatives) that my brother was ad-mitted to multiple times that was poorly staffed and offered virtually no treatment, nothing but warehousing of chronic mental patients. I remem-ber my rage and my parents' heartbreak when he came back from some of his inpatient stays with cigarette burns on his back. Bob never smoked. I have to keep these feelings and impulses in check and focus on the issues particular to the child and family in my presence and what they specifically need to heal.

I also have to work with myself every day, as Bonime did, especially as I am now in my 39th year of clinical practice, to resist the temptation when I am listening to youth and their families to think, "I've heard this story at least 500 times before." If you succumb to that way of thinking, you stop listening. You will not hear the nuances, and individual sensitivities, and idiosyncratic aspects of their experiences that in subtle and overt ways have uniquely shaped the person they have become.

I love the metaphor that Karen Horney (1942), one of the early psycho-analysts who emigrated from Europe to America, used with new patients at the beginning of analysis. She described in her book, *Self Analysis,* how she explained the process of analysis with a patient in the first session by using the metaphor of mountain climbing. Horney suggested to her patients that they could consider her an expert in mountain climbing. Continuing with the metaphor, she acknowledged that she had climbed many mountains, but she had never climbed this particular mountain. Horney further explained that if she is to successfully climb this particular mountain she will have to do it together with her patient, it has to be a collaborative effort; it will take the full participation, and committed efforts and skills of both. When I think, even for a moment, that I've heard this story before, I quickly remind myself that I've never been up this mountain before. I need to look at the particular features of this mountain, the pitfalls, drops offs, tight spots, and crevices that could pose either danger or challenge as well as the potential reward in together arriving at the top of the mountain.

I also work hard with myself and again I know where this comes from (I was so ineffective in my efforts to help my brother) to accept the fact that we will not always reach the mountaintop. During some climbs, halfway up the mountain may be all that can be accomplished and yet may result in significant gains that improve the quality of life for a given child and/or family. In some of those cases, the child or family may finish the climb to the top on their own, perhaps later in life.

In other climbs, a quarter of the way up the mountain may be considered a success because the child or family initially didn't believe they could begin the journey at all. Some of those children or families may come back later to continue the climb. This is particularly common with children who need a developmentally sequenced approach to treatment especially with regards to trauma events (James, 1989). Typically, developmental constraints require the child to do the work in steps. The child may be able to do some work at five, perhaps more work is possible at nine, and then at age thirteen they may return for still more work on unresolved grief and/or trauma because they are older and understand the impact of trauma events in a new way and have more emotional resources to undertake the climb higher up the mountain.

I have learned to take them as far as they can go up the mountain at any one time. I work with myself every day to make sure that the distance they climb is in keeping with their needs and not mine.

THE TOLLS OF A COMPASSIONATE HEART

I once supervised a highly skilled and empathic young clinician who worked in our residential treatment program. She told me one day that when she first began the work with the children, she read their stories and life histories, the all too frequent descriptions of the horrifying events in their lives of children referred for residential treatment and she was deeply moved. She found it painful to absorb. She said to me after a year working in the program that she was distressed because when she now reads such stories, she no longer has the strong emotional reaction that she experienced in the beginning. She felt she had "hardened" her emotional responsiveness not as a conscious choice, but as an adaptation to encountering this degree of horror and trauma in the lives of children. She expressed worry to me that this would make her less emotionally available to the children to hear their stories.

I believe this young clinician eloquently described the challenge to healers of children who have been severely abused and traumatized. I believe our emotional responsiveness is absolutely essential in order for us to be a healing instrument in the lives of these children. But every clinician has limits. Child therapists can easily reach the place where they rightly feel that they just can't hear one more horror story.

I remember once on a Saturday morning that I was scheduled to see a teenager who was a passenger in the backseat of a car and his best friend, also in the backseat, was killed in an accident that occurred just the day before. I had a number of trauma cases at the time in my caseload, and before going into the waiting room to meet my teenage patient I remember thinking, "I am not sure I want to hear this story." I realized I needed to do something. Balance in our lives is essential. Before I saw my patient, I called up some friends (non-psychologists) and made plans to go the next day with them on a hike in the Catskill Mountains. My friends possess an exceptional sense of humor and we laughed often, enjoyed the incredible views afforded by climbing our trail, not to mention the fresh air and the rejuvenating physical exercise.

It wasn't until discussing a preliminary draft of this chapter with a trusted colleague that it suddenly hit me how prescient my brother's words were to me. John O'Donohue (1997) suggested, "Perhaps we are only here to say certain words." Bob said, "David, have a good time." Could it be that even through the bewilderment of his schizophrenic thought process, Bob could see that his younger brother would struggle throughout his life to achieve a healthy balance?

Those therapists, who attend adequately to their own healing, nurture their own vital connections to family, friends, and colleagues and exercise care of their selves in the form of adequate rest, nutrition, exercise, relaxation and fun will be less prone to burn-out and to be more emotionally available in helpful ways to those they seek to heal. The mountains and the ocean are especially soothing and healing to me, and I regard the ocean as my "spiritual home." O'Donohue (1999) expressed my sentiments beautifully when he stated, "A day in the mountains or by the ocean helps your body unclench. You recover your deeper rhythm. The tight agendas, tasks, and worries fall away and you begin to realize the magnitude and magic of being here" (p. 202).

The support of colleagues is vital; no one should try to be a "lone ranger" in this field. Continuing education is essential since there is a rapid explosion of information and knowledge in our field, not to mention the important rewards of networking with colleagues and friends at a professional conference. I pride myself on being a lifelong avid student of psychotherapy and, in addition, to continuing education conferences which often inspire me, and renew my enthusiasm for the work, I have throughout my career sought out private supervision, most notably Dr. Bonime, and consultation with mentors and respected colleagues in the field. What works for me, may not work for you but you need a "self-care" package—you need to have a specific plan for self-care or else you will likely sooner or later suffer "compassion fatigue."

Martyrdom to the cause is not a service to anyone including our clients, let alone our families and ourselves. Sometimes I ask my adult patients when I am trying to challenge in an evocative way some self-destructive habit to write out at least five epitaphs to be inscribed on their tombstone that captures the destructiveness of their choices. For self-sacrificing therapists, some choices might be: "Here lies Dr. Dave who thought he was indispensable, so he never bothered taking care of himself. May he rest in peace, dispensable indeed!" Or, "Here lies Dr. Dave who ignored his own needs in the service of others and now is of service to nobody." If any of this applies to you, perhaps you can create your own epitaphs. Oh, the lengths we sometimes have to go to get ourselves to pay attention!

REFERENCES

Crenshaw, D. A. (2006). Family matters: In his footsteps. *Psychotherapy Networker.* (March/April), pp. 94–95.

Crenshaw, D. A. (2008). *Therapeutic engagement of children and adolescents: Play, symbol, drawing, and storytelling strategies.* Lanham, MD: Jason Aronson.

Figley, C. R. (1995). *Compassion fatigue.* New York: Routledge.

Horney, K. (1942). *Self-Analysis.* New York: Norton.

James, B. (1989). *Treating traumatized children: New insights and creative interventions.* Lexington, MA: Lexington Books.

O'Donohue, J. (1997). *The invisible world.* An audio recording. Louisville, CO: Sounds True, Inc.

O'Donohue, J. (1999). *Eternal echoes: Exploring our yearning to belong.* New York: HarperCollins Publishers.

NOTE

1. This chapter is dedicated to my mother, who at age 90+, though somewhat frail physically, is as strong in spirit as ever. She provided unfailing, loving care to my brother throughout his life. She was 73 when Bob died and both the physical and emotional demands of my brother's care were a heavy load but never once did I hear her complain. She will always be the inspiration for how I would like to live my life with no illusions that I will ever be as good a person as she.

10

Tales of Heartbreak and Joy and Reflections Along the Healing Path

David A. Crenshaw

OVERVIEW

I feel honored and privileged that my life work entails listening to the stories of countless children; children whose narratives call out for understanding; children whose pain requires witnessing; children who long to unburden; and whose voices need to be heard. It is the sensitive and delicate work of empathic and relationship healing of the wounded spirits of our children. I feel so fortunate; I can't imagine a calling more rewarding or meaningful. A few of the stories of the many children who have deeply inspired me are told in this last chapter. In the latter half of the chapter I will share some reflections regarding the healing journey spanning nearly four decades of clinical work with children, adolescents, and families.

THE STORY OF LIZZIE

Some children touch your heart deeply and you never ever forget them. Lizzie (fictitious name) was one of those children for me. Part of Lizzie's story was previously shared (Crenshaw and Mordock, 2005) but a piece of her story remains to be told, and that is the segment that I will always treasure in my heart. Lizzie, at age 9, was one of the most severely traumatized children I've ever known. I was the Clinical Director at the time that Lizzie was admitted to the residential treatment center. The Clinical Coordinator in the treatment unit that Lizzie was assigned to was on vacation at the time and so I assisted in the admission process.

Lizzie, a Child of Terror

The story previously told consisted of this terrorized child crawling under her bed and screaming at the top of her lungs upon being taken to her living group. After many attempts to get her to come out from under the bed, the staff called me to the group to help. I crawled on my stomach part way under the bed so that I could see Lizzie and I said as calmly as I could, "Lizzie, we won't hurt you. We are going to keep you safe. Kids are treated well here and you are going to be well cared for too."

Most of what I said was drowned out by Lizzie's ear-piercing screams. I heard those screams of children many times before and even more than ear-piercing, I found them heart-shattering because clearly they emanated from a deep hurt in the soul of a child. They are the screams all too often of deeply hurting children; the guttural, mournful wailing of children who have been severely, often repeatedly abused and terrified who are reliving those moments of horror as if it were happening to them right then, at that very moment and place. In my 30 years in residential treatment those screams became all too familiar to me. As of this writing it has been 6 years since I retired from work in residential treatment. I no longer hear those screams through my ears but I will always hear them in my mind. It is not something that you can forget.

When I reached out my hand to Lizzie, she attempted to bite and scratch me. I continued, "We know that this is a new place for you and it is scary to come to a place where you don't know anyone. We will keep you safe and we won't let you be hurt. You will be well fed and cared for here. Nobody will hurt you."

I offered to wipe her forehead with a wet cloth but to all my statements, Lizzie responded with still louder screams and lunges to bite and scratch me. I realized that for now Lizzie could only feel safe in this highly protected spot under the bed. So I stood up and explained to the staff in the room, "Right now, Lizzie needs to stay under the bed because she feels safe there. She may want a drink of water or a wash rag to wipe her face but she needs to be under the bed for now. Later on when she feels safe to come out from under the bed, I would like to walk her around the building and outside and show her the pool and playground and to help her to get acquainted with her new surroundings. Just call me when Lizzie is ready."

I learned a long time ago in my work with deeply troubled children that the exact language we use is powerful in its effects. I didn't say "if" Lizzie decides to come out from under the bed, rather I said "when." I didn't say "if" she would like to go for a walk, I said "when" she is ready I would like to take her for a walk. I asked one of the child care workers to stay in the room in case Lizzie needed anything and then I left to go back to my office. Two hours later the phone rang. Lizzie was ready to go for a walking tour of the grounds.

Lizzie, a Child of Courage

Over the next two weeks while her clinical coordinator was on vacation, I took several walks with Lizzie and during her 5-year stay with us in the program she made significant gains. Her treatment team did a remarkable job in the face of many discouraging moments and Lizzie's growth was amazing. Lizzie was sexually abused in her home to a degree rarely seen. From age 6 until 9, prior to being placed in our care, she had been repeated sexually violated and abused, in the period after school, by her stepfather, while her mother was at work. The stepfather threatened to kill her and her mother if she ever told, and to demonstrate that he meant business, he shot her beloved collie right in front of her.

No wonder this child did not want to come out from under the bed. But she eventually did—that is the courage of heart that is unforgettable to me and two hours later she wanted to take a walk with this male clinical director that she had just met for the first time. No wonder she was screaming in terror. But she stopped—that is what amazed me. No wonder she wanted to scratch and bite me when I reached out to her—but she didn't. That is what astonishes me about this truly special child. I saw in Lizzie that "divine spark" that James Garbarino (1999) described that exists in every child. Incredibly, that spark, that resilient spirit, was still alive in this courageous child.

Lizzie, a Child of Compassion

One occasion, I will always remember. The girls in her unit with the encouragement of the staff on their treatment team organized and planned a family day—a special day in which the families of the children in the unit were invited to come and spend a day in the program. The children with the help of the adults planned a full day of activities, they arranged for the families to visit their classrooms and meet their teachers. In addition, the girls served a nice lunch to their families and they practiced as a group several songs to sing for the families.

When that moment came and the girls stood up to sing, in the back row on the far left side was Lizzie. Lizzie had grown considerably taller over the years and she was taller by far than most of the girls. But she had grown emotionally even more. Of course, there was no family there for Lizzie to sing to. Her parents' rights were terminated and her stepfather was in jail for the crimes he had committed in his violence toward her. But Lizzie was there to sing to the families of the other girls and she put her whole heart into it. When the performance was over and the girls were milling around with their families, I took a moment to walk over to Lizzie. She smiled and asked, "Did you like the songs?" I said, "Lizzie I never heard anyone sing so beautifully because it came from your heart—and Lizzie, you have such a big heart."

I wish I could end this story on a happy note, but not all stories of such courageous and heroic children end the way we would want. Lizzie, at 14, had aged out of our program and we had to find a specialized program that served severely sexually traumatized children in her age group. We found an out-of-state facility that offered such specialized care. After her placement, on several occasions, members of our child care staff made the long trip to visit Lizzie. Reports from them and later from the facility itself revealed that Lizzie was not doing well. I suspect that even though the new program possessed the expertise, they were at a disadvantage by being a considerably larger, more institutional setting, and the kind of personalized care, attention, and concern that we provided in our program was not feasible in the larger facility.

The news was heartbreaking to all the people in our program who worked so hard for so long to turn Lizzie's life around. Do I regret that we invested 5 years of heart and soul work to reach and help this child—not for a moment and I am certain we would do it all over again if given a similar opportunity. Every child deserves our best efforts even if it is not enough to heal the deep wounds of past trauma. Every child deserves to be treated with respect, compassion, and dignity even if we are a part of their life for a relatively short time. How could we possibly give less to those who need so much more?

Lizzie, a Child of Inspiration

Lizzie will remain in my heart forever as one of my unsung heroines. She showed amazing courage, and made a comeback that no one could have expected, even if it fell short of the hoped for healing experience. The comeback she made from the first day when she would not come out from under the bed, to the day she sang with all her heart to the families of the other children is more than enough inspiration to last me for my entire lifetime. I only hope that Lizzie takes with her wherever she goes the knowledge that she will always and forever occupy a special place in the hearts of all of us who were privileged to know her.

"The Boy Who Spoke Three Languages"

In January of 1953, Sister Serena Branson, a member of the Daughters of Charities, and the first executive director of the Astor Home for Children arrived in Rhinebeck, New York with two other Sisters from the Daughters of Charities, to open the residential treatment center where I was on the clinical staff for more than 23 years of the 30 years that I worked in the residential treatment of severely emotionally disturbed children.

Sister Serena founded the Astor Home, the first residential treatment center in the United States under Catholic auspices. She later founded two other treatment centers for emotionally disturbed children, one in New York City and the other in Philadelphia and reorganized and expanded the programs of another in Albany, NY. Three boys from New York City were the first residents at Astor. One of the boys was Pete (fictitious name). When the Sisters spoke to Pete, he habitually snapped back, "Aw shut up!" After a while the Sisters grew weary of Pete's surly response. Sister Serena decided to take Pete aside to talk with him. Pete explained that he couldn't help it. Sister Serena said, "Well, how about if I teach you to say it in three other languages than it won't bother anyone?" Pete loved the idea, so Sister Serena taught him to say "Aw shut up!" in French, German, and Italian.

Sr. Serena died in July of 2003. She was a remarkable woman and was one of the most genuine, warm and caring persons, I've ever met. At the time I met her and in subsequent years she looked rather frail and thin but still full of energy and enthusiasm. I am sure she was a real dynamo in her prime. She came back to visit Astor on several occasions while her health still allowed. On one occasion, in the mid-1980s she came back to lead a staff training program and during the course of the day, I found an opportunity to talk to her about Pete.

I learned about the story originally when I was doing some research on a project related to Astor's history in the agency's archives. Sr. Serena explained that by April, 1953, there were nearly 20 children in the residence and they hired some child care staff to help manage the children. She told me that one day one of the new child care workers approached her with great excitement and told her that Pete could speak three languages. Sr. Serena said, "He can?" At that point she noticed Pete watching from the corner of the room and smiling and when she caught his eye, he gave her a big wink.

I've loved this story ever since I first read about it. Sr. Serena was able to transform this boy's status from the lowly position of being an irritant and annoyance to the group to the elevated position of being multilingual, "the boy who spoke three languages." Even more important she elevated the spirit of a boy who previously reflected his woundedness by directing his energies toward being a nuisance to others. Sr. Serena's spirit will always be ever present in the Astor programs and in the hearts of all who were fortunate to know her.

"HEARTBREAK BEYOND WORDS"

Children in foster care placement frequently suffer more than their share of losses. Typically, by the time they are placed in foster care they leave behind a trail of broken attachments that would shatter even a heart of steel. To focus on and attend to each of these losses would usually overwhelm the resources of even the most hardy and resilient child. Linda (fictitious name) somehow was able to attend to her grief although her heartbreak was beyond what any words could express.

On several occasions in my residential treatment experience, I was the bearer of tragic news and needed to inform a child that a parent, sibling, or a much loved grandparent or pet had died, sometimes under sudden and traumatic circumstances. I remember so vividly the anguish that I experienced beforehand trying to figure out the best way, the best place, the best time, and in the presence of whom, to deliver the devastating message. I know, from these anguishing experiences, there is no good way. We are unable to spare the child the indescribable pain and shock that such news evokes. If members of the surviving family can be there and actually be the ones to tell the child, this is usually far better than a clinician doing it. The clinician can be present in those cases to lend support and assistance. That was not always possible, however, given the circumstances.

The hardest of all of these experiences for me was when I had to tell, Linda, a fourteen-year-old girl, that her brother, Eric (fictitious name) with whom she was very close, had died. He had jumped out of a 7th floor window to his death. I tried to brace her by telling her that I needed to tell her something that was very hard, something that was going to be shocking, awful and heartbreaking, and then I told her that her brother had died. She let out a blood-curdling scream that I can hear to this day from the deepest recesses of her soul. And then she sobbed and sobbed. And then screamed some more. Then she pounded her fists hard into the wall. Then she just collapsed back into her chair.

I sat next to her, but said very little. If she had shown any indication that a hug would have been helpful, I would have gladly given her one. It certainly would have helped me because I felt so utterly helpless. But I took my cues from her. And I truly believe that nothing except being a caring presence was possible under the circumstances. After awhile I asked her if she would like something cold to drink. At that point her housemother joined us, a kind and loving person. And her presence was comforting to Linda at a time when her world was just blown apart. Linda stayed in my office a long time. She finally found words to tell us that she wanted to go home.

We made arrangements for her housemother to drive Linda to her home and they went to the dorm to pack her things. Before she left the office she gave each of us a big hug and we all cried together. I helped load her things in the car and before she got in the car she gave me another big hug and we cried some more. I marvel at the strength of these youngsters in facing such adversity particularly when you realize that this tragic event was the latest in a series of devastating losses that Linda had faced.

As I watched Linda and her housemother drive away for the long, sad journey home, I felt deep sorrow because I knew out that window went not only Linda's brother, but a huge part of her emotional life. She had confided in me more than once that if it weren't for the bond between her and her brother she didn't know how she would have been able to bear the horror of her life. I knew when she returned we would have much work to do and it was going to take enormous courage.

Linda, fortunately, had the internal resources and courage to do the hard work that enabled her over a period that spanned nearly 18 months of intensive therapeutic work to reconcile herself to the devastating loss of her beloved brother. When children grow up in adverse and harsh life circumstances, in Linda's case with violent and abusive parents, one of the redeeming features of such otherwise horrifying beginnings can be, but not always, a strong bond forged with siblings. Linda and her brother were unusually close, protective of each other; they hid and huddled together in fear when the rage of their parents compounded by alcohol and drug addiction was out-of-control.

Not surprisingly, there was a strong urge to reunite with her brother through her own suicide. This was a concern during the early months following her brother's death but Linda came to realize that she could best honor and pay tribute to her brother by living her life in a way that would be true to the dreams they shared.

During the worse of the family violence they would comfort each other by sharing their dreams of the future with one another. Eric was a good athlete and fantasized about playing centerfield for the Yankees. Linda was less decided, but among her dreams was being a lawyer, an obgyn physician because she loved babies, and a gym teacher. As part of her journey through grief she assembled a scrap book of clippings about her brother's athletic accomplishments. Linda and Eric once went to a Yankee game together and sat in the bleachers so Eric could be close to centerfield, the closest he ever came to his cherished dream. She had bought the tickets from babysitting money for Eric's 16th birthday. She still had the ticket stubs and put them in the scrapbook beneath a picture of the two of them at a happier time.

Linda had run away from her home after her father had repeatedly attempted to molest her. When she reported it to her mother, her mother became enraged and told her if she was going to make such ridiculous accusations she would have to find another place to live. Eric was enraged upon learning what had happened to his sister and got into a fistfight with his father; the police were called to break it up. Eric suffered undue guilt because he was unaware of what was happening and was unable to protect his sister. When Linda was shunned by relatives and no suitable foster family could be found she was placed on an emergency basis at our treatment center.

Linda proudly introduced Eric to me on his first visit to Linda at our program. He earned money as a stockroom clerk to buy a train ticket to visit Linda. He came every visiting Sunday and was the only family member ever to visit Linda while she was in our program. I once drove Eric back to the train station after one of his visits. He was far more reserved than his sister, a handsome boy, and proud of his sister for refusing to tolerate the conditions at home. Eric spent as much time as possible outside of the home dividing his time between school, sports and work. But nothing could ease his pain and guilt about the suffering of his sister and not just the molestation by their father, but also their mother choosing their father over Linda.

I saw Linda, in the fall of 2006. I gave a keynote address to the Child Life Association Conference in New York City. Linda was there and introduced herself. She is working as a child life specialist in a hospital in another city and she heard that I would be speaking at the conference. Child life specialists provide counseling, comfort, and support to young children facing serious and sometimes terminal illness in the hospital. She told me that whenever possible she returned to New York City on Eric's birthday to sit in the bleachers at Yankee Stadium. She said she can almost visualize him running down fly balls in centerfield. She said that she also believes that he would be proud of her and I told her I couldn't agree more. What a beautiful and special tribute to Eric that Linda has devoted her career to helping suffering children.

"THE GIFT OF HUMOR"

I was in the hallway on the ground floor of the residential center one day, when a child that I will give the name Julio, came running around the corner at full speed. He flew past me and out the side door leading to the back of the property. Usually when a child ran out of class or the living unit a staff member or crisis worker was not far behind, but this time I did not see anyone immediately in pursuit, so I took off after him. When I reached the outside of the building I saw him disappear over the ridge just behind the picnic tables where the children sat for barbeques in the summer time. I took off at my "full speed" which was considerably less than Julio's. When I reached the top of the ridge and started to descend on the other side, I lost my footing and slid on my backside down a steep embankment. I was shocked that this happened since it all took place in an instant.

As I tried slowly to get up and brush myself off, I saw Julio out of the corner of my eye approaching. Apparently, he had been somewhat startled by this thunderous, unbecoming slide down the slippery slope and I noticed a rather concerned look on his face when he came over to me. I think he wondered if I was going to be all in one piece and if I were going to be able to get up. When he saw that I was okay, just a little embarrassed about my lack of sure footing, he said, "Look, if you want to catch me that bad, let's go back!"

I marvel at children who have experienced so much suffering and deprivation in their lives who can still manage a good sense of humor. What a treasure, what a valuable resource to sustain you through life when you can see the comical and absurd side of life, and have a good belly laugh once in a while. I looked at Julio and then we both broke out laughing and walked back together into the school building.

"THE JOLLY GREEN GIANT" AND THE THANKSGIVING FEAST

I saw in individual therapy in residential treatment an eight-year-old boy whom I will call Jimmy (fictitious name). Jimmy loved good food and in the therapy room with me just prior to Thanksgiving he contemplated what his Thanksgiving Day feast was going to be like. He described with tremendous gusto the turkey and all the trimmings that he craved for Thanksgiving Day.

On the Monday following Thanksgiving, Jimmy looked somber when I saw him on his return to the treatment center. I learned that when he arrived at the bus stop for the Thanksgiving visit, his mother picked him up and took him to a shelter for battered women and their children. His mother and stepfather fought violently the night before his visit and his mother, badly bruised and shaken, sought refuge at the shelter. On Thanksgiving Day the volunteers at the shelter served a special meal but it did not live up to Jimmy's expectations, partly because his mom didn't prepare it and he was not at home to enjoy it with his family.

When Jimmy came into the therapy room the first thing he did was to take out all the toy pots and pans and began cooking a "Thanksgiving feast." He didn't want me to help although he allowed me to set the table. He appeared to enjoy the preparations. When he was ready to serve the dinner, he brought the food to the table and just before putting it down on the table, he froze his gaze on a baby (doll) in a high chair in the corner. He stood speechless for a moment and then he blurted out, "Oh, my God. We forgot to feed the baby!"

The forgotten baby over in the corner was Jimmy. It was the story of his life. His parents, although often well meaning, were overwhelmed with so many problems of their own, going from crisis to crisis, forgot or were unable to feed the baby, to provide the nurture, caring and protection he so badly longed for and needed.

I instinctively in a strong voice said, "It is not too late. Bring that baby over here. There is plenty of food." He immediately ran with the idea and not only brought the baby to the table, but all the puppets in the room because as he repeated over and over, "It's not too late, there is plenty of food." There was even enough food for the "Jolly Green Giant" and Jimmy invited him to the table as well. Jimmy seemed pleased with this adaptation of his story because I think it gave him hope. It at least introduced the possibility that things won't always be this way.

Given Jimmy's response, I believe that I made the right intervention and at the time, I did not question it. One of the most important goals of our work with children is to facilitate hope and to combat the demoralization they so often feel. I do, however, at this point wonder if I missed an opportunity. When he was startled by that forgotten baby in the corner was he in touch with the true circumstances of his life; that is, repeated profound loss and disappointment and did I move him quickly to a more hopeful place out of my own wish not to go into the dark pit of his profound loss and hopelessness?

As much as we would want things to get better, the circumstances of Jimmy's life might not improve. People of extreme poverty have a steep uphill climb and face many disheartening setbacks along the way. They can lose hope in the face of the constant obstacles. Was Jimmy ready to look at this and feel the pain, but I wasn't? It takes clinical courage to accompany him into his state of deep sorrow, rage and hopelessness. I still think I made the right decision given how responsive Jimmy was to the intervention, but I guess I will always wonder.

"A TALE OF FORGIVENESS"

I walked down the hall of the residential treatment center in the wing where the classrooms are located, when I heard a barely audible voice that said, "Crenshaw, I forgive you. Let's let bygones be bygones." I turned around and there was Hector (fictitious name), an eleven-year-old boy who had not spoken to me for more than 2 years. He not only didn't speak to me for that period of time but every time he passed me in the hall, he would look away and mutter obscenities as he passed. Occasionally, he mumbled threats, but I just simply pretended I didn't hear them.

Hector held a grudge toward me dating back to a Saturday night that I clearly remember. My wife and I were having dinner at a restaurant around 8:00pm with another couple, good friends, when my pager went off right after the entrée was served. I went outside the restaurant to take the call both for privacy reasons and so that I would be able to hear more clearly. The call was from the supervisor-on-call at the residential treatment center informing me that Hector had made a suicidal threat and a gesture. Even though it was not a serious attempt to hurt himself we, nevertheless, took such threats seriously because at the very least it was a communication that he was in inner pain. I conferred with the supervisor and I decided to place him on suicidal precautions and move him from the cottage he was in to the main building where the staffing coverage was more ample for the duration of the weekend.

Hector, who was prone to paranoid thinking, took this as a personal vendetta against him and was enraged with me from that night forward. When Hector, to my shock, said in a voice barely above whispering, "Crenshaw, I forgive you," I turned to him and said, "I am glad Hector, you are willing to let this go, and move on. I know it was not easy for you to do." He then turned and walked away. I was almost speechless. I was so used to Hector's mumbling under his breath profanities and threats; it was almost surreal to hear him say those simple words. I marveled at his growth and his hard work in therapy to reach the point where he could let go of a grudge that he had nurtured and tenaciously held onto for so long.

Hector was in the late stages of his residential treatment and I learned from his therapist, that Hector worked hard and long in his therapy on forgiving his mother for abandoning him. What a major accomplishment in therapy but not an easy one for any child when the most important person in his life had left him long ago when he needed her the most.

John O'Donohue (1997) in *The Invisible World* discussed how forgiveness is one of the most liberating of all human experiences. He explained in his beautiful and poetic prose how grudges are like a "hook in the heart" that drags the person along, sometimes for a long time. After his remarkable accomplishment of forgiving his mother, his therapist asked if there was anyone else he would like to forgive. It took a while but Hector struggled with removing the hook from his heart right up until the day, I heard that unforgettable soft utterance: "Crenshaw, I forgive you."

Prior to Hector's leaving the residential treatment center, he dropped by my office and though he was unable to say what most people would consider an adequate good-bye it was more than enough for me. He said, "Crenshaw, you are okay." He then reached out his hand and we shook hands. I said, "Hector, you are okay too." I wished him the best as he moved on to another program for older children and he left my office.

I appreciate how generous of heart it was for Hector to forgive both his mother and me and to make a point of seeking me out to say the best good-bye he could. I knew how difficult it was for him to let go of the deep hurt he had carried about the neglect and abandonment of his parents, and although I was in reality a rather peripheral figure in his life, his misperceptions and distorted reality led him to infuse surplus meaning in the grudge he held toward me. Perhaps my moving him to the main building for the weekend, even though the objective was to keep him safe, had reactivated deep wounds; the pain of being uprooted and moved somewhere else sometimes on short notice, a rather common occurrence in the lives of foster care children.

Whatever the source of deep hurt that my actions caused for him he still found it in his heart to forgive me, and coming from Hector, his final parting words, "Crenshaw, you're okay," is one of the finest and most meaningful tributes I've ever received. I would even be proud to have Hector's words as the epitaph on my tombstone, "Crenshaw, you're okay." What could symbolize better the fruits and rewards of a lifetime career of trying to heal the wounded spirit of a child?

HEARTBREAK AND JOY, THE TRAVELING COMPANIONS OF THE HEALER

Therapists could save a good deal of wear and tear on their souls if they retreated to a more impersonal way of relating to their child and family patients, a more cerebral approach, but in my view it would not be healing. Both mind and heart need to be present and engaged with the mind and heart of the person who seeks healing if anything meaningful is going to happen.

Readers will notice that in each of the tales in this chapter there is both joy and heartbreak. In healing the wounded spirit of a child, as in life itself, joy and heartbreak go hand in hand. Along the healing path the sweetest joy is often accompanied by devastating heartbreak. Healing is an endeavor of the heart as well as the mind, and the risks are great, but so are the potential rewards.

REFLECTIONS ON THE HEALING JOURNEY

Empathy: The Bridge to Healing Human Connection

More than a half-century of psychotherapy outcome studies have validated the essential role of the therapist-client relationship in the healing process, the tools we use matter much less (Kazdin, 2005; Miller, Hubble, & Duncan, 2007). We should not be surprised by this consistent finding from thousands of studies because it is the pain of disrupted, disappointing, neglected, and abusive relationships that brings most people to seek help, and it is in relationship with an empathic and caring person that healing takes place. The risks can be scary, the heartbreak nearly unbearable, but the joy makes the healing journey rewarding beyond compare.

Barrett-Lennard's (1981) operational definition of empathy included three different components and perspectives of empathy: the therapist's experience ("empathic resonance"), the observer's view ("expressed empathy") and the client's experience ("received empathy"). Greenberg, Watson, Elliot, & Bohart (2001) summarized the results of metaanalytic studies of empathy utilizing these three perspectives, and found that all three measures of empathy were significantly related to psychotherapy outcome.

We strive toward the goal that our work with children be informed by research based findings that guide what we do, but what we actually do, will never be pure science, but rather involves the use of the most sensitive and impactful instruments of healing, ourselves, in intimate interaction with a wounded child. The research strongly supports the notion that the quality of the therapeutic relationship has the greatest influence on psychotherapy outcome of all the variables studied. This relationship can only be quantified and formulized to a point; the remainder is intuitive and more accurately viewed as a form of the healing arts.

The work required to heal the crushed spirit of a child is intensive, indepth, emotionally focused and based on empathic and relationship healing. Establishing a relationship with severely wounded children who are often filled with rage and sorrow, and sometimes violent, is a harrowing feat. It requires an empathic attunement that children may resist because they have too frequently experienced betrayal. It requires a profound respect for their humanity and dignity and an appreciation of the complex, idiosyncratic influences that have contributed to the persons they have become.

Is the Empathic Healer a Dinosaur?

Are the days of the empathic healer numbered? Is the empathic healer an endangered species? This question was raised in the title of a thought-provoking book by Harvard psychiatrist Michael Bennett (2001). In a fast paced world seeking quick fixes to all that ails them and a managed health care system forever trying to squeeze the health care providers and patients to wring out costs to maximize corporate profits, has the heart gone out of the health care system?

Clearly, a significant number of people are helped by psychiatric medications that have been developed, especially in the last two decades, and these medications can help relieve the mental suffering of countless people. But children and youth (not to mention adults) still need and perhaps, more so in today's world, an empathic healer to listen to their story.

Children, adolescents and families will only tell their story in the presence of an empathic healer. Children, and even animals, can tell when someone really cares and when they don't and they are rarely fooled. There is no pharmaceutical remedy, no pill of any kind that can heal a hole in the heart of a child, the crushing of the spirit of youth, the most devastating of all injuries. As long as there is violence in our world, hatred among humans, poverty, crime, racial, class, gender and sexual bias; there will remain the need for an empathic healer (Crenshaw & Hardy, 2005).

Pathways to the Soul

> Eyes
> That are frozen
> From not crying
> Heart
> That knows
> No way of dying.
> —Langston Hughes

As Langston Hughes' poem (Rampersad & Roessel, 2004, p. 334) above beautifully captures, the eyes are a pathway to the soul. A popular English proverb states: "The eyes are a window to the soul." This proverb highlights that the eyes reveal what words can't always express. My favorite poet, John O'Donohue, in *The Invisible World* (1997), described how some humans, in particular he referred to men who had endured conditions of war, have seen things that no human beings should ever have to see and it is revealed in their eyes. O'Donohue observed that when you look deeply into their eyes, you will notice a deep sadness, a darkness that no light can reach. Likewise, I have witnessed that children who have suffered lacerations to the soul reveal their exposure to the dark side of life in their eyes. O'Donohue is right—you can see it in their eyes.

Human beings are capable of hiding their inner pain in an endless variety of ways but they are unable to hide the profound sadness in their eyes. It is there for us to see, if we dare to look closely. It is painful to look at that degree of sadness in the eyes of our fellow human beings, especially the eyes of children. I choose to believe that lightness can still reach the darkness deep in the souls of children and am heartened by Bessel van der Kolk's (2003) admonition, "We should assume everything is reversible until clinically proven otherwise."

A Native American proverb (Zona, 1994), expresses a corollary point of wisdom, "The soul would have no rainbow if the eyes had no tears" (p. 66). This proverb teaches us that in order to fully embrace joy we must also endure sorrow. We do not appreciate the gift of life, love, caring, friendships, health, and meaningful connections with others until sadly, we are brought to our knees by a devastating loss. But whether there is only darkness or eventually a rainbow in the soul depends not only on the inner strengths of a child or family but how much we as healers are willing to approach the darkness so that the child or family is not alone and gradually can once again let in the light.

Sealing the Fountain

One of the most poignant metaphors for understanding extremely aggressive children comes not from the field of psychology but from literature. C. S. Lewis in his book, *The Four Loves* (1965) used this metaphor in an entirely different context but it succinctly captures the heart of the pain of many children, especially those who act-out in aggressive ways. Lewis states, "They seal off the very fountain from which they thirst to drink" (p. 65). How sad, how true this is for children who adopt the strategy of keeping others at a distance by their aggressive behavior, thereby protecting from further hurt but "sealing off the very fountain from which they thirst to drink." They ensure their isolation, their disconnection, thus depriving themselves of what makes life endurable—meaningful closeness with others.

Garbarino (1999) in the *Lost Boys* noted that often we do not get close enough to notice the "traumatized child within." Bruce Perry (2006) observed in his book, *The Boy Who Was Raised as Dog*, that "by conservative estimates, about 40 percent of American children will have at least one potentially traumatizing experience by age eighteen: this includes the death of a parent or a sibling, ongoing physical abuse and/or neglect, sexual abuse, or the experience of a serious accident, natural disaster or domestic violence or other violent crime" (pp. 2–3).

Sometimes we don't see the "traumatized child within," "the invisible wounds" or the "fawn in the gorilla suit" because we become inducted in the overly punitive climate that permeates our culture. When these children are already broken down in spirit does it make sense to subject them to even harsher and more punitive correctional methods? Hardy (2004) stated, "Children need less correction, and more connection. They need less confrontation, and more validation."

Goethe once said, "We see in the world, what we carry in our heart." John O'Donohue (2004) in *Anam Cara* stated, "The human eye is always selecting what it wants to see and also evading what it does not want to see" (p. 62). Our society has not always distinguished itself by its treatment of children. The first case of child abuse to be prosecuted in this country in the 1890s was done under statues protecting the welfare of animals since there were no such laws at the time protecting children (Haller, 2002). Fast forward to 2007 and what is our collective response as a culture to the sexualization of young girls, if we look carefully we will notice this taking place at younger and younger ages.

How is it that as a collective we don't notice the inner pain that drives the acting-out behavior of our children? How sad that so many children in today's world miss out on the childhood that each and every child deserves, a time and place of safety, when trust and security in the world can develop, a time for joy, laughter, and play. In the absence of healing relationships with committed adults today's lonely and alienated youth will continue in their desperate attempts to protect from further hurt, to "seal off the very fountain from which they thirst to drink."

The Poetry of Play

Children's symbolic play like poetry is remarkable in its ability to condense in rich metaphor what is important to be expressed and understood. I regard poetry as play with words and play as poetry without words. It never ceases to amaze me how young children can tell so succinctly the stories they need to tell through their pretend play. A child, for example, who grew up in poverty and missed out on even the basic nutrients that most take for granted, may come into the play room and set up a grocery store in pretend play. The child is the grocer and the therapist is asked to be the customer. When the customer arrives, the door is slammed in his face, and sign is put up on the front of the door that says in big black letters: **"Closed."** The customer is told in less than polite terms to come back tomorrow. When the customer arrives at the store the next day, the same thing happens. The feelings of the therapist are instructive when the door is slammed in his face, and told to come back another day, only to have the same thing happen. The therapist begins to experience in a small way what it has been like for this child to be turned away repeatedly, to have the door slammed in his face over and over, when seeking to satisfy even the most basic needs in his life. After all, it was a grocery store, not a luxury goods store that was repeatedly closed to him.

This is what I refer to as the "poetry of play"—play that is poetry without words. Like poetry and all forms of art there is always something left out in children's symbolic play for the reader or observer to understand—the dots are not all completely connected, there is an unfilled space, a missing piece that invites the other to engage in a creative way with the poetry with words or the poetry without words. Children's play like other forms of poetry are open to different interpretations, meanings, and the emotional resonance and impact will vary from one observe to another depending on how the dots are connected and what missing piece is inserted into the creative puzzle.

The Uninvited Guests ("Ghosts") in the Therapy Room

Walter Bonime in psychoanalytic supervision instructed me when the therapy process bogged down to ask my patient a compelling question: "What is it that you don't want to talk about?" The answer to that question invariably held the key to the impasse.

In every therapeutic encounter whether individual, family, or group, I've learned to appreciate a powerful, unannounced, secret participant. Paradoxically, the poignant presence is absence. Although silent, the unacknowledged absence is articulate; an organizing force that calls out in a variety of ways to be recognized. The absence is personified by the stories not told, the secrets guarded, the feelings, topics, and issues avoided, the people living or dead not there but who occupy a central place in the emotional life of a child, family, or group. This phenomenon is popularly referred to as "the elephant in the room."

One of the most important decisions the therapist will make in the course of therapy is whether or when to announce the unacknowledged ever present guest. In bringing the hidden life of the child or family into the open, the dark and secret undercurrents into the light, to give voice to the unmentionable is a matter of great delicacy that requires utmost sensitivity to timing, pacing and readiness to accept the unveiling of the secret member in the therapy room. Great care and thought must be given to both the beneficial and potentially adverse consequences of this dramatic intervention. It is almost guaranteed that it will be a highly emotional, perhaps transformative moment in the healing process.

Relational Empathic Healing

> The art of therapy is about making connections including connection with self. The more connections we have, the richer our lives.

> —Olga Silverstein (1995)

Olga Silverstein captured the essence of what Relational Therapy is all about—expanding connections, repairing ruptures, opening up the disconnections whether within the family, the larger community, within the therapeutic relationship or even in relation to self. It is the meaningful ties we have with others and ourself that makes life worthwhile and bearable even in the worst of circumstances.

Relational, empathic healing emphasizes the therapeutic relationship with the child or family and the collaborative nature of the journey.

> Come walk with me
> Don't despair
> I will accompany you

Together we will find the path
That leads to your place of healing and belonging.
—David Crenshaw

If we are able to make a meaningful difference in the life of a child, it may influence the kind of spouse, parent, grandparent, friend, boss or colleague that child becomes in adult life and that influence can reverberate for generations to come. We can contribute in a modest way to creating a better world—by making a meaningful difference in the life of at least one child or family. It is a brief opportunity because the window for making a healing connection with a particular child may close quickly. It is also brief, because as healers we share in the human condition that we are on this planet on a temporary visa that could expire at any time. For the empathic healer, there is no greater gift or opportunity; no greater joy than when we extend a compassionate heart, a helping hand to a lost and wounded child or family. Children come into this world possessing that unique specialness that Garbarino (1999) called the "divine spark"—may that divine spark in our children never be extinguished.

REFERENCES

Barrett-Lennard, G. (1981). The empathy cycle: Refinement of a nuclear concept. *Journal of Counseling Psychology, 28,* 91–100.

Bennett, M. J. (2001). *The empathic healer: An endangered species.* San Diego, CA: Academic Press.

Crenshaw, D. A., & Hardy, K. V. (2005). Understanding and treating the aggression of traumatized children in out-of-home care. In N. Boyd-Webb (Ed.), *Working with traumatized youth in child welfare* (pp. 171–95). New York: Guilford Press.

Crenshaw, D. A., and Mordock, J. B. (2005). *A Handbook of Play Therapy with Aggressive Children.* Lanham, MD: Jason Aronson.

Garbarino, J. (1999). *Lost boys: Why our sons turn violent and how we can save them.* New York: Anchor Books.

Greenberg, L. S., Watson, J.C., Elliot, R., & Bohart, A.C. (2001). Empathy. *Psychotherapy Theory, Research, Practice, Training, 38,* 380–84.

Haller, L. H. (2002). Overview of child forensic psychiatry. *Child and Adolescent Psychiatric Clinics of North America, 11,* 685–88.

Hardy, K. V. 2004. *Getting through to violent kids.* Presentation at the Psychotherapy Networker Symposium. Washington, DC.

Kazdin, A. E. (2005). Treatment outcomes, common factors, and continued neglect of mechanisms of change. *Clinical Psychology: Science and Practice, 12,* 184–88.

Lewis, C. S. (1965). *The four loves.* New York: Harcourt Brace.

Miller, S., Hubble, M., & Duncan, B. (2007). Supershrinks. *Psychotherapy Networker, 31,* 26–35.

O'Donohue, J. (1997). *The invisible world.* An audio recording. Louisville, CO: Sounds True, Inc.

O'Donohue, J. (2004). *Anam Cara: A book of Celtic wisdom.* New York: Perennial.

Perry, B. D., & Szalavitz, M. (2006). *The boy who was raised as a dog and other stories from a child psychiatrist's notebook.* New York: Basic Books.

Rampersad, A., & Roessel, D. (Eds.) (2004). *The collected poems of Langston Hughes.* New York: Knopf.

Silverstein, O. (1995). *Inclusion/Exclusion.* A presentation at the Ackerman Institute for the Family. New York.

Zona, G. A. 1994. *The soul would have no rainbow and other Native American Proverbs.* New York: Touchstone Books.

Index

About the Contributors

David A. Crenshaw, Ph.D., ABPP, is director and founder of the Rhinebeck Child & Family Center, LLC in Rhinebeck, NY. Previously he was Clinical Director at the Astor Home for Children and the Rhinebeck Country School devoting 30 years of his professional career to the residential treatment of seriously emotionally disturbed children. He is Co-Founder and past President of the New York Association for Play Therapy. Books he has authored include: *Evocative Strategies in Child and Adolescent Psychotherapy; Therapeutic Engagement of Children and Adolescents;* and he has co-authored with John B. Mordock, *A Handbook of Play Therapy with Aggressive Children* and *Understanding and Treating the Aggression of Children: Fawns in Gorilla Suits.*

Susan Cristantiello ATR, LCAT is an art psychotherapist and serves as the CCSI Coordinator for Astor Home Based Services in Dutchess County, New York. She has been in private practice for over twenty-five years, and has been a professor of Art Therapy at the College of New Rochelle and Westchester Community College. She was one of the founding members of the Westchester Art Therapy Association, were she served as President, Vice-President and Program Chair of the chapter. She has contributed to the American Art Therapy Journal, lectured widely, and has worked as a lecturer, consultant, and training supervisor throughout her career.

Andrew Fussner, MSW has worked 30 years as a family therapist; 20 years at the Philadelphia Child Guidance Clinic. He currently works as mental health consultant to the pre-k—kindergarten head start program of the

School District of Philadelphia, adjunct faculty at the Graduate School of Social Policy and Practice of the University of Pennsylvania, and consultant in family therapy at the Astor Home for Children in Rhinebeck, NY.

James Garbarino, Ph.D., holds the Maude C. Clarke Chair in Humanistic Psychology and is Director of the Center for the Human Rights of Children at Loyola University Chicago. Previously he was Elizabeth Lee Vincent Professor of Human Development and Co-Director of the Family Life Development Center at Cornell University. Books he has authored or edited include: *See Jane Hit: Why Girls Are Growing More Violent and What We Can Do About It* (2006), *Lost Boys: Why Our Sons Turn Violent and How We Can Save Them* (1999), *Raising Children in a Socially Toxic Environment* (1995).

Kenneth V. Hardy, Ph.D. is recognized as one of family therapy's preeminent teachers. He is also a passionate and powerful advocate for social justice, whose cutting-edge work on the challenges for clinical practice posed by race, ethnicity, and poverty is internationally recognized. He is co-author with Tracy Laszloffy, Ph.D. of *Teens Who Hurt: Clinical Interventions with Violent Youth*. He is considered an international authority on the dynamics of oppression. Much of his work is devoted to examining the intersection between the various dimensions of diversity including race, class, gender, sexual orientation and the process of therapy.

Linda Hill, LCSW-R, CT is a licensed clinical social worker practicing in the Mid-Hudson Valley region of New York State. She completed her post-graduate education at Smith College School for Social Work, specializing in the clinical treatment of children and adolescents. She is also certified in the field of Thanatology: Death, Dying and Bereavement through the Association for Death Education and Counseling. A Fellow of the New York State Society for Clinical Social Work, she actively serves on the board of the Society's local chapter and co-facilitates its peer consultation group. Ms. Hill maintains a private practice in offering psychotherapy and grief counseling services to children, adults and families.

Jennifer Lee earned her Ph.D. from Teachers College, Columbia University. She completed her clinical internship at New York Presbyterian Hospital and her post-doctoral training at the Astor Home for Children. She is currently a psychologist in the Astor Home for Children's School-Based Program. She is a member of the American Psychological Association, the Hudson Valley Psychological Association, and the New York Center for the Study of Groups, Organizations, and Social Systems.

Konstantinos Tsoubris, Ph.D. is an assistant executive director for the As-tor Home for Children. He is responsible for the programmatic oversight of the community mental health programs that serve children and families in Dutchess County, New York. He is a graduate of Hofstra University where he received his doctorate in clinical and school psychology. He is also an adjunct professor in the Behavioral Science Department at Marist College.